How to Win
The Future of Law with
Artificial Intelligence

How to Win
The Future of Law with Artificial Intelligence

Isabella Barbara Tisenhusen

Bloomsbury Professional
LONDON · DUBLIN · EDINBURGH · NEW YORK · NEW DELHI · SYDNEY

BLOOMSBURY PROFESSIONAL

Bloomsbury Publishing Plc
50 Bedford Square, London, WC1B 3DP, UK
1385 Broadway, New York, NY 10018, USA
Bloomsbury Publishing Ireland Ltd
29 Earlsfort Terrace, Dublin 2, D02 AY28, Ireland

BLOOMSBURY and the Diana logo are trademarks of
Bloomsbury Publishing Plc

First published in Great Britain 2025

1

Copyright © Isabella Barbara Tisenhusen 2025

Isabella Barbara Tisenhusen has asserted her right under the Copyright, Designs and Patents Act 1988 to be identified as Author of this work.

All rights reserved. No part of this publication may be: i) reproduced or transmitted in any form, electronic or mechanical, including photocopying, recording or by means of any information storage or retrieval system without prior permission in writing from the publishers; or ii) used or reproduced in any way for the training, development or operation of artificial intelligence (AI) technologies, including generative AI technologies. The rights holders expressly reserve this publication from the text and data mining exception as per Article 4(3) of the Digital Single Market Directive (EU) 2019/790.

While every care has been taken to ensure the accuracy of this work, no responsibility for loss or damage occasioned to any person acting or refraining from action as a result of any statement in it can be accepted by the authors, editors or publishers.

All UK Government legislation and other public sector information used in the work is Crown Copyright ©. All House of Lords and House of Commons information used in the work is Parliamentary Copyright ©. This information is reused under the terms of the Open Government Licence v3.0 (http://www.nationalarchives.gov.uk/doc/open-government-licence/version/3) except where otherwise stated.

All Eur-lex material used in the work is © European Union, http://eur-lex.europa.eu/, 1998-2025.

British Library Cataloguing-in-Publication Data

A catalogue record for this book is available from the British Library.

ISBN:	PB	978 1 52653 274 9
	ePDF	978 1 52653 276 3
	ePub	978 1 52653 275 6

Typeset by Evolution Design & Digital Ltd (Kent)
Printed and bound by CPI Group (UK) Ltd, Croydon, CR0 4YY

For product safety related questions contact productsafety@bloomsbury.com

To find out more about our authors and books,
visit www.bloomsburyprofessional.com. Here you will find extracts,
author information, details of forthcoming events and
the option to sign up for our newsletters.

Preface

In the true fashion of a lawyer, this is more of a disclaimer than an introduction.

This book explores the evergreen concept of a lawyer working with a client. The book also demonstrates how lawyers can make use of AI tools, and how such tools can make our daily work so much more rewarding.

You are welcome to read this book from beginning to end, or any of its individual parts that interest you. The book is written in a way that would enable you to dive into whatever topic you are interested in. Feel free to refer to the Table of Contents to guide your reading.

In writing this book I drew inspiration from my own experience as a lawyer, and also the experience of colleagues who were very kind to talk to me. However, it is necessary to note that any references to any clients and cases are purely fictional.

Reference to AI tools in the book includes language models, generative AI and any other technical tools that make use of machine learning, as available at the time of writing. AI and its implementation are considered from the point of view of a lawyer and not an engineer, which I am not. Therefore, technical jargon has been deliberately kept to a minimum throughout the book.

This book does not include the latest news around AI, simply because with the current rate of technological advancement such info would become redundant by the time you read it. Having said that, various AI tools were used in researching for the book and also in writing its appendices. I have attached Appendix 2 at the very end listing some of them. Please feel free to refer to it throughout your reading and try out various AI tools listed there.

Please feel free to connect with me as you are reading this, and share your thoughts on the future of our profession!

I hope you enjoy the book.

Isabella Barbara Tisenhusen
Find me on LinkedIn.
For professional enquires, email isabella@tiesenhausen.fr

Acknowledgements

Thank you to everyone who took the time out of their busy days to share their thoughts on where our industry is going or otherwise inspired me to embark on the path of writing this book. Special thanks to the following:

Deelika Ljaš

Imbi Jürgen

Joanna Rindell

Daniela Solano Palacios

Barbara Walshe

Danielle Benecke

Yrjö Ojasaar

Marcus Bagnall

Omri Bouton

Rob Cant

Nicholas Crossland

Mark Deem

Charles Kerrigan

Richard Mabey

Raj Mahapatra

Tom Marshall

Luke Pardey

And most of all – my always supportive husband Paul without whom none of it would have been possible. Thank you for your endless belief in me and thanks for all the writer's snacks!

Finally, I want to also acknowledge the law firm where I started my career – Sorainen. Most of what I know about being a 'good lawyer' I learned

Acknowledgements

early on in my career while there. I was lucky to work with some of the very best lawyers – especially Toomas Prangli, who always demonstrated integrity and set the bar very high in terms of helping clients succeed. To this date, if I am faced with a challenging situation, I think 'what would Toomas do'? Thanks for being my North Star.

Table of Contents

Preface   *v*
Acknowledgements   *vii*

PART I: WHAT DO CLIENTS NEED?   **1**
Introduction   1

Chapter 1 Clients need to be able to trust their lawyer   **3**
1.1   Core client need for trust   3
     Clients come to us in stress   4
1.2   How to build trust with clients   5
     Why responsiveness matters   6
     Communication is key   6
     Mutually beneficial relationships   7
     How to restore trust when it is broken   8
1.3   How AI can help us build trust   9
     Saving time on lower level tasks   9
     Completing work more effectively   10
     Prioritising human interactions   11

Chapter 2 Clients need to be able to rely on their lawyer   **13**
2.1   Core client need for support   13
     Clients have a lot going on   13
     The essence of legal support   14
     The burden of getting to clarity   15
2.2   How to make clients feel supported   16
     Providing clear answers   16
     Tailoring our legal advice to client needs   17
     Keeping our work papers to ourselves   18
     Sending status updates   19
2.3   How AI can help us provide better support   19
     Refining our message   20

Chapter 3 Clients need to save legal costs   **21**
3.1   Core clients need to save cost   21
     Current billing model   21
3.2   How to be cost savvy   22
     Getting to the right value proposition   23
     Win-win arrangements   23
     Keeping clients informed of fees   24

Table of Contents

3.3	How AI can help us be more cost savvy	24
	Is AI going to take our bread away?	25
	How to bill work done by AI	25
	Other side of the billing situation	26

PART II: NEW GENERATION LAWYERS — 29
Introduction — 29
Introduction to AI tools — 31

Chapter 4 Lawyers as language engineers — 33
4.1	Dealing with the written word	33
	What kind of writing style serves our clients best?	34
	What does clear legal drafting look and sound like?	35
	What is not clear legal drafting?	36
	What actually helps clients?	37
4.2	How to write better with AI tools	38
	No more 'blank page block'	38
	Cure for the 'template fallacy'	39
	Contracting, but better	40
	Infinite use cases for AI	41

Chapter 5 Lawyers as data processors — 43
5.1	Conducting legal analysis and drafting documents	43
	How our brains work	43
5.2	How to analyse and draft better with AI tools	44
	How language models work	44
	Using AI for transcribing meetings	44
	Using AI for research	45
	Risks involved in using AI for research	47
	Using AI for contract drafting	48
	Using AI for project management	50
	Using AI in litigation	51
	Using AI in depositions and discovery	52
	AI-powered dispute resolution	54

Chapter 6 Lawyers as therapists — 55
6.1	Empathy towards clients	55
	Delivering difficult messages	55
	Understanding the client's core issue	57
	Personal cost to lawyers	58
	Lawyer mental health issues	58
	Being constantly 'on'	60
	Typical day in a lawyer's life	61
	Steering client expectations	63
6.2	How to be more empathetic with AI tools	64
	Getting the tone of our message right	64

Table of Contents

	Getting our first reply out quickly	66
	AI first responder	67

PART III: NEW GENERATION LAW FIRMS — 69
Introduction — 69

Chapter 7 What does a new generation law firm look like? — 71
7.1	Putting the client back in the centre	71
7.2	Talking to clients in a way that speaks to them	72
7.3	Building relationships instead of selling	73
7.4	Building a personal brand	74
7.5	Servicing all client needs	75
7.6	Taking care of the firm's main asset – lawyers	76
7.7	All law firms need to keep up with technological innovation	77
7.8	Every lawyer needs to understand Web 3	78
7.9	New generation law firms are powered by AI	81
7.10	How to work with AI as a lawyer	82

Chapter 8 Phases of AI adoption at law firms — 85
8.1	Shorter term changes	85
	Current status of legal review	86
	Improved legal review with the use of AI	87
	Fully utilising AI in legal review	88
	Human vs machine: risk profile	89
	Current status of contracting	91
	Improved contracting with the use of AI	91
	Human versus machine: numbers	92
	Other tactical responses by law firms	93
	What kind of AI tool is useful for a lawyer	94
	What kind of AI tool is safe to use as lawyer	95
	How to implement the use of AI at law firms	96
	Phases of implementation of AI at law firms	96
8.2	Longer term view	97
	Training a law firm AI	98
	Approach to training an AI	99
	Building custom AI solutions for clients	103
	AI assistant as the 'first responder'	104
	Pushing work on someone versus pulling work for yourself	106
	Issues with pushing work on someone	107
	Why pulling work for yourself is much better	108
	Lawyers want to be winning at the game of law	109
	AI assistant for case management	110
	Future law firm structure	111

Chapter 9 Tasks that will remain with human lawyers — 115
9.1	Relationship building and management	116
9.2	Understanding of nuances, context and ethics	117

Table of Contents

9.3	Human expertise and creativity	117
9.4	Problem solving, strategising and negotiations	118
9.5	Marketing and sales	120

Afterword: Advice to young lawyers — **123**
Learn from the best — 123
Start by being helpful, in order to become valuable — 124
Find your field — 125
Adopt a client service mindset — 126
Adopt a daily practice to reflect — 127
Try out different career paths — 127
Avoid the 'specialist trap' and the 'law firm trap' — 128
Going for a partner, or not — 129
Legal career outside law firms — 130
Increasing areas of expertise — 130
Use AI as your second brain — 131
Navigating in uncertain terrain — 132

Appendix 1: AI-generated executive summaries — **137**

Appendix 2: List of AI tools useful for lawyers — **139**

Index — *167*

Part I

What do clients need?

INTRODUCTION

As true professionals, we are constantly obsessed with finding the right answer to a legal question and delivering it in a beautifully drafted document. However, as we pursue that, we may lose sight of what really matters. Yes, we need to know the law and give proper legal advice to our clients, but we also need to remember that we are in the business of servicing clients. So, before we even start with new generation lawyers and law firms, it is crucial to touch upon what our clients need. If our clients had no needs, then we would have no work. And if lawyers had no work, there would be no law firms either. Only if we properly cater to the core needs of our clients, can we have mutually beneficial relationships and a level of retention that perfect legal writing alone will not bring.

Whereas the daily needs of our clients are somewhat different in the current technology era, the core needs have remained fundamentally the same throughout the decades. If anything, such core needs may have become even more pressing, as meeting such needs seems to be in short supply. Everyone is busy, everyone is online, no one really has time to give appropriate attention to one another. It is therefore necessary to emphasise that our clients are still human beings, and they have very human needs – and such human needs can be catered for by human lawyers. Therefore, it is us, lawyers, who can build trust with our clients – and it is us, lawyers, who can make sure our clients feel supported.

Having said that, the advancement of AI is bringing about a true renaissance for lawyers. Now we have a plenitude of powerful tools that we can use to take care of the 'heavy paper lifting' part of our work – and thereby, hopefully, free us up a bit more for interacting with our clients, building human relations and delivering appropriate services, while also making us feel more rewarded in our daily work. Because it goes both ways – a happy and appreciative client will tend to make us feel more fulfilled and therefore happier as well.

Let us now explore the core needs of our clients and how we can improve our value proposition to them by becoming more conscious of such needs, and by fully utilising the technology available to us today.

Chapter 1

Clients need to be able to trust their lawyer

1.1 CORE CLIENT NEED FOR TRUST

Professional service providers – like us, lawyers – need to build trust with their clients. It is extremely important.

Trust is a human bond that we form in relation to each other. If we do not have trust, our professional advice may fall flat regardless of how good it is. Lack of trust undermines everything else, even excellent legal advice. Why should a client take the advice of a lawyer that he does not trust?

The irony is that we study so hard to become 'good lawyers', but we hardly ever think about human nature. And then we get into our legal practice and all we do is provide advice to other human beings. We focus on the technicalities of the law, ignoring the nature of our activity – which is that of service providers. We are so obsessed about doing a good job and we are constantly rushing to meet deadlines, but we often neglect to take into account that doing a good job includes more than just getting the content of our legal advice right.

If we did not have clients, we would not have work. And as long as our clients are humans, we need to work with human nature.

A lot of good professionals neglect the importance of interpersonal skills. However, to become a partner at a law firm, we need to win clients over to the firm. To win clients, we need to be outstanding service providers. And to be outstanding legal service providers, we must be great in building trust with clients – because, ultimately, clients decide whether to give us work or not, and this decision is primarily based on whether they trust us or not.

The essential elements for becoming a fully rounded lawyer are as follows:

| Studying and practising law → | Building relations with colleagues and clients → | Learning about business → | Becoming a good lawyer → | Mastering human nature → | **Becoming a fully rounded lawyer ...** |

Clients need to be able to trust their lawyer

So, all of us should be looking to build sustainable relations with our clients over a long term. Every seasoned lawyer knows that the best client is a repeat client that the firm is able to service in a comprehensive way, with regards to all of the client's needs (and also those needs that are yet to be discovered). A repeat client brings a stable level of fees and usually also buys services from other teams of the firm, therefore becoming a steady source of income for the firm.

Clients come to us in stress

Clients often need their lawyer to help them out in a high-stress situation. Therefore, they need to be able to reach out to us and consistently communicate with us, in order to bring a level of comfort into an otherwise stressful situation and to feel supported by us.

Nothing has changed in this respect at the client end. At our end, admittedly it has become increasingly more difficult for our clients to reach us and to be able to rely on us in their moment of stress because we tend to be consistently busy, scheduled back to back and generally overworked. So we sometimes drop the ball on being there for our clients.

Instead of being able to reach us in their moment of need, the client now has to leave us a voice message, send an email to request for a call back, and wait in line after all of the scheduled back-to-back meetings ... or, if in luck, perhaps secure a virtual meeting spot with us for the next day. The next day? The next day!

We sometimes push the needs of our clients to the end of the line, because we are simply too busy doing all the important legal work – which is of course very important, but we should try and remember that the actual work of a lawyer is to service clients. So if we do not give attention to our clients in their moment of need, we fail on the most important task.

It may be easier to ignore our client than to deal with whatever they have going on at a time that really does not suit us. But such an approach may backfire. We may find ourselves having more work later on to calm our client down. Or perhaps the situation the client is in has become worse while we did not prioritise picking up the phone. It may even be our client themselves that escalated the situation because they were not able to rely on our professional guidance when it was needed. Ultimately, we are also risking losing our client to someone else who prioritises their needs better.

How to build trust with clients

Responsiveness is key here. A quick acknowledgement of the client's situation and offer of some level of support or at least an indication when the support would be available. It does not mean jumping at everything the client sends our way, it simply means noticing them and acknowledging their existence in their moment of need. We will come back to that throughout the book.

1.2 HOW TO BUILD TRUST WITH CLIENTS

Communication is key in building trust with our clients.

A seasoned lawyer knows that it pays to quickly respond to a new client request. In a sense, a new client request is like an invite to a date – so we should let them know that we got the invite and signal that we are looking forward to it. Almost like we have been waiting for it all day, even though we have been working hard and barely noticed it coming in.

Such responsiveness signals that the client matters to us. That their business matters to us. That we want to be in partnership with them. No one likes the feeling of anticipation after extending an invitation. To anxiously wait until the other has nothing else to do and finally brings themselves to reply to you.

Sending out a request for legal assistance is a key moment for a client. They have realised that they need help. And they have decided to turn to us for help. This is the moment when we need to be able to respond promptly and bring our assurance into the matter. A short reply to the client's first enquiry suffices in most cases. Simple 'got it and happy to help'. That takes less than a minute.

Responding quickly to client requests for critical services is of utmost importance. Let us imagine it like this – you are walking on the street minding your own business, but all of a sudden you fall down and do not manage to get back up. You struggle to get your footing, maybe you even hurt yourself. After a moment, you realise you need help to get back up. So you look around and raise your hand towards a passerby who looks reliable. You are holding up your hand and trying to get their attention. You want them to acknowledge that you need their help right now. Not tomorrow, or the day after. Now.

What our clients need at the moment of first enquiry is for us to acknowledge that we notice them and are able to help them. Just the acknowledgement that they exist, and our readiness to help them. A nod of the head in their direction, if you may. A nod that would signal that we are on the way, that help is on the way. At this moment our clients do not need a ride into town. Or a comprehensive map of all the possible routes. They just need to know we are there to help them.

Why responsiveness matters

Being in the legal business is like being on the dating market. Appearing worthy and approachable. Arriving on time and keeping promises. Ensuring our value by delivering what was agreed. Not neglecting to call back. Not being late for a meeting without a timely apology. Not making an appearance while wholly unprepared.

When was the last time you saw your client in person? If that was more than six months ago, you should not think that you are still their trusted lawyer. They may be sending you work still, but the moment a new 'cool' lawyer comes around, the once steady relationship may be jeopardised. This may happen to relationships of any kind if they have been neglected on a human level. Which inevitably means putting in some actual person to person time.

In the current technology era, we have moved away from the personal assurance a lawyer brings into the matter, towards a more fast-food type of legal advice where the chef that cooked the meal does not matter much. While the 'legal fast food' will likely get better with the use of AI, there is a real competitive advantage to be gained by lawyers who are more close to their clients.

Yes, we are so busy working. But let us remember, we would not have any work if we did not have clients in the first place. Seeing our clients face to face will give them the much needed human assurance that they can rely on us. This cannot be underestimated. This also cannot be replaced by a machine.

Communication is key

It is similarly important to keep our clients informed as the matter we are handling for them progresses. For us this may be one client amongst many that we are working with at any given moment. However, for our client this may be their most pressing legal issue that keeps them up at night. So they will want to be in the info-flow. We should therefore send regular updates to clients. And if a client asks us a question, we should reply.

Communication goes both ways. It should not be too burdensome for clients to reach us and our simple reply should not take too long. After all, we live in a time of instant messaging. This has conditioned us to expect quick communication.

Communication is especially helpful for our clients in high-stress legal matters. We may not always have enough sensitivity towards what constitutes high-stress for our clients, as we deal with legal matters every day. Therefore, it is better to rather over communicate than to neglect communication. To illustrate the point, let us look at another profession that also often deals with clients who are stressed – dentists. Imagine going to the dentist with some kind of pressing ailment, opening your mouth and then the dentist just does their work without a word to you. While you sit there not knowing what is going on, with various tools drilling away in your mouth, and all the unpleasantness that comes with it. How does it make you feel? Now imagine another dentist who first discusses your situation with you thoroughly, sympathises with you, and once working on it keeps you informed of everything that goes on in your month, while also consistently checking in with you 'are you okay'? Which one is a better client experience? Which dentist would you go back to in the future?

Communication is a powerful skill for building trust with our clients. It also comes with an added benefit for us. If we consistently keep the client informed of how the matter is progressing and what kind of work we are doing on the matter, the client will be more understanding when they receive our bill because they already know the hard work we have put in, so there should be no surprises. We may also find that if we sympathise with our client's situation, they may also be more accommodating to us – for example, when we fall sick and need to postpone a meeting with them. If we have built mutually respectful relations, they may not even chase us during our vacation (provided that we use an out of office responder!).

Mutually beneficial relationships

There is certain satisfaction in helping clients. There is a certain pride in doing good work and getting immediate appreciation for it. Most lawyers are driven by challenges and overcoming them. Therefore, having more direct communication with clients will provide us more immediate feedback and also help us feel happier in our profession. After all, we are all 'social animals' whether we like to think so or not.

Mental health issues among lawyers are on the increase and there are so many unhappy lawyers all around us (especially in the Big Law). Perhaps that is partly because we have lost the human connection with our clients. We have turned into keyboard lawyers, cogs in the machine, and it just does not have the same level of satisfaction as presenting our beautiful legal solutions in front of a real-life client and seeing their appreciation in real time.

While we need clients in order to have work, clients also need us because the legal topics they deal with are complex. That is a great foundation for win-win type of relationships. If we build trust with our clients and provide good counsel, then clients will want to turn to us if a new legal need arises. The more we put attention into creating such a virtuous cycle, the better time we will have at work. Because we will have good rapport with our clients, we will have work coming our way, and that allows us to excel at what we do.

Law is a long game and there are a lot of potential clients in need of our services. And they talk to each other. Our reputation often precedes us. Therefore, how we treat our clients tends to reach very far. Similarly, if we are super communicators we will have many doors open to us. Good words of our clients can take us very far indeed.

> *While I love doing deals, some of my best moments as a lawyer have been with clients – seeing that they appreciate my work. It has made me feel like I am accomplishing something. That I have an effect on the world – through helping my clients achieve more and better. I tend to remember some of my favourite clients very well. We spent some good time together working on hard things and it was very rewarding.*

How to restore trust when it is broken

Restoring trust is much harder than building it in the first place. However, if we have had a mishap with a client, this brings a good opportunity to restore, and even strengthen, the trust we have. As the saying goes – you see the character of a person when something goes wrong. And something will go wrong, that is just part of the job.

If we made a mistake, the best way to approach it is to talk to the client openly and admit that. This opens up the avenue to get to the bottom of the situation and try to find a solution – to the legal situation at hand and also to repairing relations with the client. Most clients will react well to a lawyer admitting to their mistake, as long as the admittance is immediate and transparent.

We all make mistakes, yet as lawyers we have this self image that we need to be infallible. Sure, we need to do everything to avoid making mistakes or minimise them at least, but the reality is we will make mistakes. And the best way of dealing with them is to face them, and not try to ignore them by shovelling them under the carpet and pretending that nothing happened, or coming up with the most amusing excuses.

Lawyers who dare to admit their mistakes and to have an open communication around them with their clients, may very well see that these clients will trust them even more. Because admitting one's mistakes is hard, and only someone with integrity (and therefore someone trustworthy) would be able to do that.

1.3 HOW AI CAN HELP US BUILD TRUST

First of all, AI tools can help us with our clients in an indirect way. If we make good use of the latest tools, they will help us with the 'heavy paper lifting' of our daily legal work. This in turn hopefully frees us up to see our clients a bit more. To be the face in front of the client again.

Saving time on lower level tasks

Let us look into it more precisely. On an average day, a senior private practice lawyer will likely spend around 10–20 per cent of their time on legal research and analysis for on-going client matters, around 40–60 per cent on providing legal advice and services to clients, around 10–20 per cent on client communication (responding to enquiries, sending fee quotes, providing matter updates, etc), and the remaining time on miscellaneous things like entering timecards.

As mentioned, on average around 10–20% of a senior lawyer's time is spent on legal research (for junior lawyers this is easily double). Legal research tends to be a time-consuming task – we have to determine the right materials to find answers from, get hold of them, and spend a lot of time getting to the answer.

Clients need to be able to trust their lawyer

In the Internet era and with the digitalisation of legislation, practice manuals and case law, we have been able to get to the answer much faster. With the use of AI tools, we can get to the answer in seconds.

So here is a reason for all of us to start using these potent tools – to get to the answer faster. To spend less of our time on research tasks. And to free up some of that precious time to consciously build relationships with our clients.

While we cover AI tools in detail later in the book, here is a brief introduction to the subject.

AI tools suited for legal research and analysis need to be trained on a collection of data specific to the particular research field. Such tools should also be able to check the online resources relevant for the particular task in real time (eg, latest legislation). And they should be trained by other lawyers in terms of methodology of getting to the right answer (while eliminating any issues like hallucinations, biases etc).

As an example, an insurance litigator in Florida would be best served by an AI tool that has the knowledge of the relevant legislation, practice notes and case law. And that can verify for any latest updates in real time. Just like a lawyer would. Added to this is the user-friendly interface of AI tools. In our example, the Florida lawyer will want to ask AI questions the same way they would ask them from another colleague – while remembering that quality questions bring quality outcomes.

As we work with an AI tool, we essentially ask it to do things for us – to find answers, write up memos, sort out our initial thoughts and further refine our thinking.

Feel free to refer to **Appendix 2** for specific AI tools suitable for legal work – research, analysis and drafting. Try out several of them and find the one that best serves your specific needs. We will touch upon each of the use cases in more detail throughout the book.

Completing work more effectively

As demonstrated, we spend the majority of our time on providing legal advice and services to clients (around half a day or more). That is the bulk of time spent (and billed) for providing legal services to clients. It may consist of writing up a legal opinion, managing a transaction, or negotiating a contract. Whatever the specialisation, a majority of a lawyer's time is spent on legal advice.

Again, with the use of AI tools we can be so much more efficient here. It takes time to think things through, analyse factors, and refine our thinking. We can cut down some of that manual processing in our brains and essentially brain dump our notes and initial thoughts into an AI and ask it to refine them down and provide a quality outcome.

There are infinite ways of making use of various AI tools in our day-to-day work as lawyers, and the possibilities are ever expanding in line with the rapid emergence of new tools. We will thoroughly cover it in the book, but for now, let us assume an unforeseen increase in productivity with the use of AI.

Prioritising human interactions

AI or no AI, let us never lose the very human connection with our clients. Because in the end, this is what we will remember. We will forget the size of the deal, but we will always remember that we saved the day when it almost fell apart. And we will remember that phone call where a freaked out client had been magically transformed into the most appreciative and relieved person ever. Thanks to us. That in itself can be extremely rewarding.

Similarly to us, our clients will forget the specifics of legal advice we gave them (unfortunately). But they will remember that they were able to rely on us. They will remember that we helped them. So, should they need any help in the future, they will come to us. And they will recommend us to other potential clients.

The best sign of a client's trust is referrals to new clients. Sometimes these potential clients do not even fall within our professional expertise. That may mean that we have been so good at building trust with our client, that they recommend us to everyone they think might need a lawyer. And because we were able to make them feel supported, they think we can help anyone. In anything. That is the essence of being a trusted advisor.

Chapter 2

Clients need to be able to rely on their lawyer

As noted in the previous chapter, communication is a number one skill for any professional service provider. But communication alone is not going to cut it if it does not come with the necessary support. Clients need to be able to rely on us as their legal partners, not mere service providers that keep a comfortable cushion between themselves and the client.

2.1 CORE CLIENT NEED FOR SUPPORT

Let us look into the perspective of an inhouse client working with various outside counsels. There are hundreds of outside counsels available, and they are all very smart. So how do you stand out? For many clients, it comes down to whether they feel supported by us. And support is a comprehensive matter, we need to tick all the boxes here. However, it becomes almost self-fulfilling once we adapt the mindset and intent of actually wanting to support our clients. This means removing the cushion between us and them.

Supporting clients starts with communication – clear, quick and consistent. Letting the client know that we got their request. It also means summarising complex legal matters in a short note. Updating them on the progress of the matter we are working on. And not leaving them hanging and wondering what is the status of the matter they trusted with us.

But real support also means offering our personal view as if we were in their shoes. And calling them to deliver bad news personally instead of a surprise email. Also, keeping the agreed fees under check and letting them know of deviations in advance. All of this may sound obvious, but we do not always do that. We get carried away in our day-to-day work. Too busy to make our clients feel supported. Too drained of energy and attention.

Clients have a lot going on

Allow me to speak from personal experience here to illustrate what goes on with our clients.

Clients need to be able to rely on their lawyer

When I worked at a law firm as a transaction lawyer, I used to have up to three big deals going on simultaneously, or five to ten smaller matters to handle for different clients.

When I went inhouse as a general counsel (GC), I had so many legal and non-legal topics to handle, I could not even tally up how many projects I had on the go. If I tried to estimate that number now, it would perhaps be around 30 to 50 at any given moment with different priorities, risks and stakeholders.

A GC generally has the board to advise, the C suite to partner with, and the legal team to manage. Added to this are all the overlapping matters with the finance team, sometimes also HR. A GC usually keeps oversight of all major transactions and contracts, while also steering a couple of litigations on the side if necessary. And at any given moment someone might reach out across the organisation asking for support in whatever they have going on. And these are all different matters, big and small, across business and legal. While some GCs do rely on a legal team, it is often not the same level of reliance they would expect from an external counsel.

So, a GC may need to trust some of their legal matters with an outside counsel. Their main need here is for the outside counsel to help them carry some of the workload, and remember to do that so that they do not have to. That means ownership of a matter that has been trusted outside. And a great level of ownership, better than the client would get inhouse (otherwise they would not turn outside).

Clients need us to bring comprehensive support into the matter. To make their lives easier and not even more complex.

Now, given that, if I wake up one morning and while standing in the shower remember that I gave an important legal matter to an outside counsel to handle, as my trusted and well-paid partner, but despite trying hard I cannot recall the latest status of the matter – this erodes trust. This is where I do not feel supported, and need to reach out to see what the status of the matter is. What is going on? Can I rely on you?

The essence of legal support

Clients need practical legal support – it needs to serve some actual business need that they have. If it does not, then a beautiful legal writing is likely to have no value to them.

Core client need for support

Sometimes we tend to make our clients' lives unnecessarily complicated. For example, we may add a lot of assumptions and disclaimers to our regulatory advice. Now these assumptions and disclaimers often put the responsibility back on the client. So for a client, instead of being reassured on their regulatory remit, they still have to worry about where they stand. We are not really helping clients if they are still left with a considerable level of uncertainty.

We write out the assumptions and disclaimers mostly because of our own risk mitigation. We are so worried about any liability for the things we write to our clients. And sometimes it just goes too far. Our clients need us to take a reasonable level of responsibility for our opinions. This is often why they pay us – to take their worry away, in order to bring some level of certainty into their otherwise uncertain situation.

Business owners and managers are already carrying a lot of personal risk and liability in relation to their business. Much more than a regular private practice lawyer ever will. And when they come to us for legal advice in a particular matter, they expect us to take this one thing off of their chest. And they pay us for doing that. Yet, we sometimes fail to deliver. We may send them a beautiful memo, but still leave them wondering where they stand in the matter.

The burden of getting to clarity

Another thing that we tend to do, often unwillingly, is bury the answer so deep underneath the facts, assumptions, disclaimers, citations, etc. We may get carried away in our legal analysis, eager to show all the hard work we have put in, but on the flip side we leave the client with the burden of getting to clarity and finding the answer they are looking for. Not very helpful.

Our clients should not have to read 20-page long memos on complex legal topics going round and round in circles, making their hairs stand on end and trying to anticipate which way it will land. And they may get to the end of it and not understand a thing! And it may happen even if they have a law degree, because we have presented a complex matter in a complex manner, leaving them to do the work of trying to understand what exactly we are trying to say here.

Our clients should not have to spend extensive effort in reading our long-winded text, trying to find answers relevant to their situation. But often this

Clients need to be able to rely on their lawyer

is exactly what we make them do. We send them our collection of smart thoughts and let them dig into it. There are many, many, clients doing that this very second. Yes, we have provided our learned opinion. But have we actually made their lives easier? Have we brought much needed clarity into whatever situation they are dealing with?

And what if our client does not have a law degree, how are they supposed to even manage? We should not be surprised if some of them just take a glance at the memo, put it in a drawer and pray.

2.2 HOW TO MAKE CLIENTS FEEL SUPPORTED

Every smart lawyer can write a long memo on a complex legal topic in beautiful, well-rounded language and with never ending sentences and present it to the client to figure out the hidden message. It almost takes a lawyer to work with a lawyer, but it should not be the case!

Only the best lawyers are able to explain a complex legal topic in a short note that any busy business person is able to quickly grasp within 20 seconds. The best tax memo that has ever existed is on one page and is worth ten times its size in gold. The best restructuring plan that has ever been presented consists of one graph that explains the whole complex undertaking. Only when understanding the matter fully are lawyers able to put forward work with such clarity.

Let us try and imagine stepping into the shoes of a client that is seeking regulatory advice; their company begins to operate in a new territory and they are not certain what business they are allowed to do, yet they still have to personally carry the risk of any regulatory breach (willingly or unwillingly, there is no escaping that).

Now, say they turn to an outside counsel to guide them in these unclear waters and in return receive a detailed legal analysis of 20 pages, full of nuances and no clear yes or no. They do not really have time to read all of this, yet they are worried, so they have to. All they wanted was help from a knowledgeable professional. All they got was more work for themself.

Providing clear answers

A significant part of a lawyer's work is about (i) getting to the answer and then (ii) presenting the answer in a useful way to the client. Our clients

How to make clients feel supported

do not always appreciate how complex law is and that we sometimes do not have the answers right there and then. We need to get to the answer. Meaning we need to research and analyse to find the right answer (or answers) that work best in the current situation.

Now, once we have done the first part of the exercise and found a presentable answer, we need not neglect the second part which is presenting it in a way that is helpful to the client. In complex topics, how we present something is as important (if not more) as the answer itself.

We cannot expect our clients to be interested in reading 20 pages of legal text. Beautiful legal text, yes. But still 20 pages of text. That is not serving the needs of our clients. Yet, this is what we sometimes do as lawyers. Shipping extensive legal analysis into our clients' mailboxes. And then we bill them for it.

As an industry we tend to think that the content of the legal advice is all that matters, and the more complex our content, the smarter we look. But in order to effectively help our clients we need to uncover their core needs around the issue, any relevant factors affecting the issue, and then try to help them with the actual issue at hand the best we can and in the most appropriate way they need.

Tailoring our legal advice to client needs

Allow me to bring an example from my private practice. (You will see examples of our daily work throughout the book in the indented text style like below.)

> A new tech company came to me in need of terms and conditions (T&Cs), despite having already received beautifully crafted T&Cs from a reputable law firm which they felt a bit uneasy about. Their feelings were that the T&Cs just did not reflect well on their innovative product, and so they did not feel comfortable putting them in front of their users and partners. The T&Cs were simply too complex, full of legalese, full of detail – very hard to follow. Not helpful, confusing even.
>
> As I was very interested in their product, I had taken time to understand how it worked. What is the user journey? What are the different use cases? This enabled me to take the long-form T&Cs, work out what each section meant in the context of the product, and then rewrite them in a way that the average reader would be able to follow.

Clients need to be able to rely on their lawyer

> And guess what? The client was absolutely amazed by the revised text after all the rewriting and getting to the essence of the matter. Finally, they were able to understand WITH EASE what was written in their own terms and conditions! And they felt like their users could also understand and rely on this useful information. That helped to create a roadmap for their users and partners to understand how their product worked.

I can go on endlessly about clear legal writing. There are so many ways of doing that if we just put our mind to it. We can use chapters to structure the text. We can title the chapters in helpful self-explanatory ways for ease of reference. We can use clear language. We can use short sentences. We can use plain words. The list goes on, and on. And we will keep coming back to this topic in the book.

Keeping our work papers to ourselves

Let me try and illustrate a related point from a different angle. As a transaction lawyer, I have sometimes found myself doing restructuring when the market happens to be down. In such situations I have worked with clients that have a complex corporate structure, often cross border, and a long list of issues why the current structure does not work (eg, risk mitigation, tax, competition concerns).

Corporate restructuring is an engaging exercise, because it involves so many different variables and they are all more or less connected to each other. In dealing with many variables and interconnected factors, it helps to start mapping them down. Therefore, I have spent a fair amount of time drawing structures. With pen on paper, I would draw many sketches looking at how everything stands right now and played through various scenarios of how the structure could be moved around.

Now my point is, my clients never saw these drafts. I kept them in the drawer. What they saw was a clear graph on the proposed final structure (sometimes with an alternative). And then we would look at that together, and through our discussions test that it truly worked from their perspective.

Financial and tax advisors use a similar approach. This is also why legal design is very useful. It helps to bring the relevant information to clients in a shape and form that is more self-explanatory, instead of sheer volume of text. Good legal design helps to convey a complex topic in an easy-to-comprehend and intuitive manner. Most complex legal matters could benefit from design prior to being presented to the client.

Sending status updates

We can expect that our clients are busy and lack internal resources. This is why they come to us for help. We can therefore also expect that they do not have resources to manage us on top of all the other people, stakeholders and matters they need to manage. They need us to manage them. To take care of them. To simply provide them occasional updates on the progress of the matter (and the fees incurred, which we will discuss in more detail in the next chapter). So that they feel reassured that we are on top of it and can have their peaceful morning shower.

It takes two minutes to send a status update. If we do not have two minutes or we think it takes more, we need to improve our time management skills and effectiveness.

2.3   HOW AI CAN HELP US PROVIDE BETTER SUPPORT

Did you know that we misunderstand each other once every other minute that we interact? This means that when we deliver legal advice to our clients, for example, over a video meeting, every other minute they will misunderstand something we say. That is how bad we are as humans in communicating to each other. Partly that is due to all the 'background noise' that we each have in our heads, to try and make sense of the world around us.

Now, there are three main consequences to miscommunication: (i) the client may ask us to explain something they did not quite get – great, we can iron out the wrinkles in our message, (ii) we may realise we have been ambiguous and self-correct our message, or (iii) the client misunderstands us and takes away something that is not correct on the face of it being our legal advice (the absolute worst!).

These very human communication issues are why we should be looking forward to a personal AI agent that would speak for us with our client's AI agent, free from our personal backgrounds, knowledge gaps, brain scatter, language barriers – and make sure the message gets across. So, in the future, it may very well be the client's agent that is communicating with the law firm's agent, and it is fascinating to consider what this means in terms of improving communication between us.

Clients need to be able to rely on their lawyer

Refining our message

But before we get further into the future, let us embrace what AI tools already offer us. As noted before, we, lawyers, are famous for our long-winded literary writing. We learn it at law school and we read it in practice papers. We take great pride in our professional style. Yet, it is not commercially feasible for our clients. Our clients should not expend considerable effort and time in order to understand the essence of our legal advice.

It takes time to refine our text down to a clear message. It is much easier to put forward long-form text (some of it copied and pasted perhaps from a source material that is often the worst in terms of writing style – ie, the law).

And then we argue at court over the meaning of a clause in a contract. That is the bread and butter of thousands of commercial litigation lawyers. This is how ambiguous our legal writing can be. But it should not be so.

We should instead aim for crisp and clear writing. Short, concise sentences. Not too many specific terms that our clients would have a hard time deciphering. This is where AI tools can be extremely useful. AI tools can help to reduce some of the professional jargon in our writing. They can give us a powerful shortcut into making improvements to our legal writing.

AI tools can help us refine our thoughts and writing, and bring out the essence of our legal advice with the level of clarity our clients will appreciate. So, a good approach is to process our writing through an AI tool and ask it to improve the text for clarity, before we send it out to the client. We can also ask the AI – is it clear enough? Please repeat back to me what is the essence of my message.

Please refer to Appendix 2 for various AI tools that include message processing functionality and can indeed be very useful in improving our legal writing. A good approach to start with would be to take a general AI model, feed in a section of complex legal text, and ask it to improve the wording for clarity and conciseness. Why not take a complicated legal wording from a piece of legislation and feed it into ChatGPT and see what happens?

Chapter 3

Clients need to save legal costs

3.1 CORE CLIENTS NEED TO SAVE COSTS

While legal advice is not necessarily something to scrupulously save on when it comes to operating a business, there is an ever-increasing price pressure on law firms. From the client's perspective, it is important to justify the value their inhouse legal function and outside spend brings to the business. And such value is often not clearly evident. In sales, for example, it is possible to demonstrate the pipeline and revenue. Whereas legal value often lies in risks that did not materialise – for example, the transaction that did not go haywire because it was well managed, the commercial partner the company did not lose because they were well taken care of, the legal claim that the company did not receive, etc. In many ways, proper legal function is like an active insurance against any material risks, and also an enabler for the business to grow and thrive.

Most clients have a strict budget for buying external legal advice. That is something they need to take into account and manage. There will be competing needs for these resources. On the other end, most lawyers have billing targets that they need to meet. That is something they need to work hard towards achieving. For a long time that has been one of the main metrics of a lawyer's value to the firm.

Now, while we can expect the legal fee structures to move further away from hourly billing towards agreed fee scopes, filling up this quota on one end and dealing with limited resources on the other end is a very innate battle when it comes to legal cost.

Law firms need to find a way to remain profitable in an environment where we are expected to do more with less time spent. Therefore, we need to leverage technology to deliver our services, essentially to achieve more with less lawyers (and less cost to the client).

Current billing model

On average, private practice lawyers aim to bill between six to eight hours per day (while in the 'Big Law' the numbers can be much more). This figure includes legal work and various activities associated with providing legal advice.

A significant part of a private practice lawyer's day is spent on research, document drafting and review – what I like to call the 'heavy paper lifting'. This is at the core of the traditional legal work where we sit and review documents, look for answers in legislation, draft legal opinions, etc. It is all related to processing information for some desired outcome.

The proportion of such processing work depends on the lawyer's seniority. Junior lawyers in large law firms may spend more than half of their time on research, document review and other processing tasks, while senior lawyers spend more time on problem solving, strategic thinking and client interactions.

Overall, it can be estimated that an average lawyer spends about three to six hours a day on various data processing tasks, which include document review and legal research. That is three to six hours each day spent processing data!

Many things could be said about the current billing model itself, but for now, let us just note that it is long overdue.

3.2 HOW TO BE COST SAVVY

The best approach we can take as outside counsels is to try and work within the budget that our client has agreed to.

It is on us to make sure that we are selling the right services to the right client for the right price. If we do not take this into account it will backfire sooner or later (eg, the client will not pay our bill because they did not get the value they expected). The best lawyers know that, and willingly admit when they are not well placed or well prized to provide certain legal advice. And the clients remember that. (This is actually a great way of building trust with a client.)

On the other end of the equation, it is also up to the client to try and find the best lawyer for the matter and to try and get the best out of them for the best possible price. That takes some effort and practice, but it is possible to find the right lawyer with the right value proposition for any given legal situation.

Getting to the right value proposition

A lot of work can be done outright to eliminate the chance of disappointment in the fees down the line. The best lawyers are very upfront on their fees, they keep an open communication with their clients providing regular fee updates, and are willing to switch gears if it makes more sense to their client.

When it comes to billing, the guiding principle should be – what is this worth to the client? This should steer our thinking and be the foundation of all fee arrangements. Billing time has been a metric to represent value, but it can go wrong if we are billing time for something that the client actually does not appreciate.

A good approach is to try and imagine ourselves in our client's shoes. If you were them, would you continue this particular litigation with a mediocre chance of recovering the claim and part of the fees, while destabilising the entire organisation, or would you actually settle and concentrate on growing the business? The best litigation lawyers know when to settle and save their clients years of agony down the line. Now, they will lose out of their fees in the short term. In the long term, having good intent towards clients will advance their reputation on the market, and they will have more work coming towards them.

Whereas, the worst external counsels will try to lure the client in with their impressive accolades, try to say as many smart sentences as they manage, and then once working on the matter try to bill as much as possible by over complicating matters and moving in roundabout ways, making the whole situation appear as complex and expensive as possible. While it may bring in some more fees in the short term, in the long term it damages their reputation and clients will steer away from them.

Win-win arrangements

Early on in my practice, I realised that win-win really is the best arrangement in client relationships. If my client 'wins', I too 'win' down the line. In the short term I may lose out on some of the fees, but that is alright because I keep building trust with my client. In the long term, this same warm contact may send me a case that is bigger than I ever expected. And it may bring in more revenue than the first case ever did.

Clients need to save legal costs

Whereas those lawyers who try to squeeze every penny out of every client, will always have the burden of doing that and this becomes their daily reality. While those lawyers who take a fee cut here and there where it does not make sense to charge their client more, or perhaps refer a case to their colleague if they are not best placed to handle it themselves, those lawyers seem to always have work, from good clients, and usually with good fee arrangements. So which one has a better day to day?

If client satisfaction is low, our bills may be left unpaid. Having upfront and clear fee discussions with our clients is a must for a sustainable relationship. Being clear on the fees is a great way of building trust with clients, while also making sure in the first place that what we are providing is worth its price for the client. By doing that, we will have much less complaints about our fees and much better collection times.

Keeping clients informed of fees

As noted, it helps to keep our clients informed of the fees in advance and never go over budget. If circumstances change and we see that we may go over the budget, we should discuss it with the client in advance. Perhaps they are fine, or perhaps we need to adjust the fee scope. We never know what internal considerations the client may have (eg, they may be going through a restructure and therefore having to keep all costs under tight control). Communication is key here.

The best lawyers also send their bills out themselves with a quick personal note. It works well for them, because it is much harder to neglect and not pay an invoice sent to you by an actual person, who happens to be the same person that has treated you well and helped you by providing some useful advice to you. It introduces reciprocity into billing and we humans are prone to follow it. It also allows the client to voice any complaints they may have directly, and not let them accumulate over time and thereby potentially damage the relationship.

3.3   HOW AI CAN HELP US BE MORE COST SAVVY

As discussed above, a lot of hourly fees consist of time spent on researching, drafting and other data processing tasks. The bulk of this can be done more efficiently with the use of the right AI tools. This frees up some of the attention for lawyers to concentrate on where it matters the most – bringing in the necessary quality assurance to the legal advice prepared, and making sure it gets delivered to the client in a helpful manner. Please refer to **Appendix 2** for specific AI tools.

Often complaints about lawyers being too expensive has got nothing to do with the lawyers being too expensive, but is simply a result of using the wrong lawyer in the wrong place – where it does not make business sense from the perspective of cost spent versus value brought. It is on us to explain the value of our services and make sure that we provide them to the right clients in the right way – so that we are effectively servicing their needs that are worth the money we are asking for. Introducing AI into the equation is just another facet of that.

Is AI going to take our bread away?

Lawyers that fret that AI is going to take our bread away simply need to start using AI and bring their practice to a new level. With the use of AI, we will be able to service more clients, better.

Having said that, we can expect our clients to demand that the efficiency we get from using the latest tools is also reflected in our billing as appropriate. The drive to save fees on the client end will never end, it is simply part of market forces.

So, perhaps AI will finally kick us out of the hourly billing model, for good?

How to bill work done by AI

The revenue model of law firms is based on human lawyers recording time, which is then billed to the client. If we add an AI into the equation, and have it do part of what has been traditionally considered a lawyer's work, then the lawyer will presumably bill less time to the client, thereby potentially raising the need to somehow bill the value created by AI to the client. Or does it?

Initially, it may be that individual lawyers will not disclose their use of AI and thereby not reflect the effectiveness they received thanks to it on their timecards. Instead, they may bill their time as usual for any given task, even though they were able to complete the task faster. So they are personally reaping the benefits.

Clients need to save legal costs

As time passes and adoption increases, we may expect law firms and their clients to be more open to the use of AI by lawyers. At this stage, law firms may attempt to find a clever way to bill some of the cost of the AI tools to their respective clients.

As the adoption increases even more over time, and clients start to expect the use of AI tools by their savvy lawyers, the prices for data heavy tasks are prone to decrease. Once the clients understand sufficiently that the bulk of the work can be processed by an AI, they may not be willing to pay for the human power equivalent for this work. This would drive the overall project fee down depending on how much of the work can be done by AI, and how much still needs to be completed by a human lawyer.

At the same time, more enterprising law firms may start introducing their proprietary AI solutions, and bill their clients for them. Who knows, maybe we will even see a standard for an 'hourly fee' work done by an AI, or a fixed fee for using a certain service the law firm has developed, perhaps even a retainer? In any case, the use of AI will bring an excellent yet challenging opportunity to finally rethink the billable hour model that does not often serve the interests of our clients.

As law firms are going to need less of the traditional human power, and will be utilising more of the latest technology, they need to consider where their value proposition to clients is and how they charge for that. A significant part of the human labour will be undertaken by AI tools with much more capacity, so the firms would be losing out on that part of the billing. At the same time, if we are able to rethink our business model and value proposition, we can elevate our service to a whole new level.

Law firms may be forced to rethink their financial model, because with the increasing use of AI by lawyers and their clients, interesting questions emerge. For example, how do we bill our work to the client when the majority of the work was done by AI that the firm uses? Similarly, a client may ask why the firm is billing them for a work that can easily be done by AI? Firms need to keep in mind that many of their clients are using and will increasingly use AI tools themselves.

Other side of the billing situation

We can also expect our clients to use AI to analyse our bills. They can pool all of our timecards together and compare various metrics against the market and their other legal providers. This would give the client a position

How AI can help us be more cost savvy

to come back to us and ask – why did we charge 20 per cent more than last time for this particular matter? Or, why are we charging more overall than our competitor that the client also uses?

Data is power, and our clients already have a lot of data on our invoicing. They have years' worth of bills stacked up, with countless pages of timecards. All they need is to analyse the data in an effective manner. So firms need to be ready to have these conversations.

Part II

New generation lawyers

INTRODUCTION

Richard Susskind said in 2015 that 'lawyers will in large part be replaced by advanced systems, less costly workers supported by technology, or by lay people armed with online tools'. Well, we certainly seem to be getting there.

I am very happy to be a practising lawyer during the era of knowledge revolution. It has never been more exciting to be a lawyer. Finally, our centuries long traditional profession is going through some real rapid change! We are seeing a big shift towards new technologies in our industry, which enables us to change our old ways of thinking of the law.

When I first went to school, we started off with no computers whatsoever ... We dragged our heavy paper books and took sloppy handwritten notes. We sent letters to our international pen pals by post and patiently waited a week or two for their reply.

Then we learned to use the first desktop computer to do fun things ... And learned to do document processing on a computer. And learned to use email (and started to send emails instead of letters to our pals!).

Oh yes, at some point we were also obsessed about faxing documents all across the world.

Somewhere along we got our first laptop and started dragging it everywhere with us ... We started to handle 10 ... 50 ... 100 emails per day. Until we got the iPhone, and started to handle 10 ... 100 ... 1,000 instant messages every day. Our phone has been glued to our hand ever since.

And now we are learning to use AI.

I wish we had scanned our brains throughout these technological advancements. They must have grown some seriously amazing neural pathways to facilitate all of this.

New generation lawyers

I firmly believe that AI will entirely reshape the legal profession, both private practice and inhouse. We are only starting to wake up the potential of this technology.

AI will reshape how we study law, how we approach legal matters and how we deliver legal advice. It will, on the one hand, make legal knowledge easily accessible for the average person, while on the other hand, turn lawyers into project managers and communicators. Because if the answer is easily accessible, then what is left for us lawyers to provide?

We are left with the fundamentals – finding out what are the actual core needs of our client, asking the AI the right questions to get to the right answer, vetting the answer and delivering it with our professional assurance attached to it.

The new generation lawyer is therefore a great communicator, strategist and project manager. They are also great at fully utilising the new technology available to them and keeping up with the latest developments. They have the necessary technical understanding to check the build and reliability of different AI tools to vet them for a particular use.

All of this is as inevitable as emails. In today's world it is impossible to be a lawyer and not use email. That was not obvious a mere decade ago. The same will happen with AI.

Dear reader, you can sit back and relax and let the future unfold. Or you can be on the new frontier and participate in the making of the future. The choice is yours.

We know that the legal industry moves relatively slow compared to other industries, and especially when it comes to technological advancements. But it does not exist in a vacuum, it will inevitably be influenced by new technologies and it will pick up useful new tools.

And let us also remember – we are all surrounded by younger colleagues. They were born with iPhones in their hand. They will be the ones who will happily lean into various AI tools. Because why ask a grumpy older colleague when you can ask chatty ChatGPT?

We already know that younger generations prefer to work differently to us. They do not necessarily want to meet us face to face. They may prefer video calls. And they certainly prefer to work remotely. So it is very much in line with their way of work to use AI instead of a human mentor.

Introduction to AI tools

With the advent of so many AI tools, tech skills are becoming necessary also for more senior lawyers. We cannot ignore new tools, instead we need to learn and adapt. Please refer to **Appendix 2** for a variety of AI tools.

One of the core skills of a future lawyer is the ability to synthesise information across platforms. That will be the foundation of our legal work. On top of that we would be exercising our executive function in making good use of the pre-synthesised information. This is where we will bring in our expertise and seniority.

INTRODUCTION TO AI TOOLS

Before we get into specific use cases for AI, let us look at the various functionalities of currently available AI tools. Please refer to **Appendix 2** for a selection of AI tools useful for lawyers.

Broadly speaking, at the time of writing this book, AI tools can be divided into two main categories: (i) productivity tools and (ii) practice-specific tools. Let us look at each of these more closely.

Productivity tools enable us to increase our standard productivity. In this category we have various AI enhanced tools for searching, summarising, drafting, etc. The function of these tools is to, for example, help search for answers in a more effective manner, or help us summarise a large volume of text. Even help us get started or improve our drafting of documents. The purpose of such tools is essentially to enable us to do what we already do, but do it faster and better.

Practice-specific tools are those that are tailored for our specific professional needs. There are AI enhanced tools for commercial lawyers, litigation lawyers, for any kind of lawyers really. Similarly, there are specific tools for project management that have been tailored for lawyers (eg, due diligence software that enables us to manage the specific legal project much more effectively).

On top of these two main categories, we can expect more custom-made tools to emerge. They can be custom made for a particular law firm, or for a particular team within the law firm. Similarly, they can be built to meet certain needs of a type of client, or even just certain needs of one key client.

New generation lawyers

Preferably, any AI tool that a lawyer uses in their practice, would have an input from other lawyers in their development phase. Or at least be quality controlled prior to professional use. In law, we deal with certain risks and we abide to certain standards, therefore we would want to make sure that they are met to an acceptable standard before we use an AI tool in our professional work. More on that later in the book.

Chapter 4

Lawyers as language engineers

4.1 DEALING WITH THE WRITTEN WORD

As lawyers we deal with the written word every day. We are the ultimate 'language engineers'.

We are looking for answers from a written text, be it legislation or contract. As we go about it, we are also synthesising 'what we read' with 'what we know' about our client's matter. And we do all of that with the goal of getting to an eventual work result – an answer to our client's question. Such an answer will again be in a written word for our client to read and take in.

Every lawyer knows that the choice of the right word is crucial. There is a vast difference even just between synonyms, as some of them may come with a heap of legal meaning, whereas others may not. For example, to act 'with due diligence' and 'in good faith' means to fulfil a variety of legal requirements. All very familiar concepts to lawyers, covered in a variety of legislation and court cases. So these notions are packed with meaning for lawyers. Whereas to act 'with good care' and 'sincere intent' gives very little legal context.

As we have been carefully processing words ever since the first lawyer was accepted to the bar, we have learned along the way to take great pride in our impeccable writing skills. This has resulted, as an example, in a writing style which can sometimes be truly Shakespearean. Some might even say flowery.

In historical context, our style of oral and written argument originates primarily from ancient Greece, enriched by Roman legal practices. The integration of rhetorical techniques from Greek philosophers and the procedural formalities established by the Romans has shaped the modern legal landscape, influencing how lawyers craft and present their arguments today.

Great orators, philosophers and politicians have come before us, and have set the foundation to a learned discourse. Even though we have moved far

Lawyers as language engineers

as a civilisation ever since, our profession tends to still be somewhat rooted in similar aspirations.

Let us think about the repercussions of using such a style from a client's perspective.

What kind of writing style serves our clients best?

Elaborate writing style with carefully crafted sentences that go on forever and ever between meticulously positioned commas, albeit beautiful to read as a literary masterpiece and certainly a masterful use of the English language, can have an adverse effect on our clients and counterparties, as at worst such a writing style can be difficult to follow by the average reader, making it hard to comprehend and therefore commercially unfeasible in delivering our brilliant legal advice, since the client on the receiving end of such advice may not actually understand what is it that we are trying to say, and therefore may unwittingly neglect to take our advice, or in the worst case misunderstand it wholly and proceed in a way that was not advised by us.

Long and complex writing can be beautiful, but is often confusing to clients.

Did you notice the difference?

In some cultures, there is a strong custom of adding niceties and politeness around our written correspondence. This takes some getting used to, but usually does not take away much from the matter at hand, but instead wraps it in a lovely package. However, when we think in terms of providing written legal advice to our client to act upon, or drafting a contract to be presented to the counterparty, the style of our language becomes critical.

Every lawyer has a story about a contract that was written, negotiated and signed, but then became a subject of dispute between the parties as a certain term within it had suddenly became impossible to understand or at least arguable. Many contract disputes evolve around what the parties' intention was in agreeing to 'this' or omitting 'that' in the contract. How do we end up like that, while being such masterful language processors?

One might argue that this is due to our sometimes archaic and complex writing style. A style that even lawyers find difficult to interpret. But does it have to take a lawyer in order to understand a legal contract written by another lawyer? Not necessarily.

Lawyers are meant to support businesses. But businesses do not consist of only lawyers, instead they mostly consist of people with different qualifications from us. While admittedly the legislation has consistently increased in complexity, and therefore it often takes a lawyer to decipher it, we should not necessarily add to the existing complexity. Instead, we should aim to solve it for our clients and counterparties, and try to find sufficient clarity in every given situation.

Some of the best lawyers are able to put forward legal documents which include such a level of clarity that the reader is able to follow their train of thought upon first reading. However most legal text takes several attempts to get to its message. Over the course of my career, I have come to greatly appreciate the former and advocate against the latter. Especially after having spent years on the receiving end of complex legal compilations.

When did we drift so far from simply writing down the arrangement between the parties, and instead created a hurdle that is the legal contract of today?

> *I have over the years sought to adopt a style of writing that is clear and concise. The legal teams I have worked with know that I have implemented 'drafting guidelines' outlining a drafting style that is easier to follow for the reader. Clear writing does not always come naturally to us as lawyers (and to this day, I sometimes fall short on my own requirements). However, I firmly believe it to be a path worth taking as at the end of it we will find sufficient clarity in terms of any given legal situation. We will also find contracts that are easily negotiable and understandable for the people who need to execute them.*

What does clear legal drafting look and sound like?

If we want to test our legal writing for clarity, we can read it out loud to ourselves and ask – does it make sense what I am saying here? Sometimes we find ourselves stopping midway having lost our train of thought. And sometimes we chuckle at vocalising the archaic words we have written. But more often than not, such an exercise makes us realise the unnecessary complexity of our text.

Why do we tend to write so differently from how we speak?

Lawyers as language engineers

Another good test is to consider whether a third person would be able to understand our text upon first reading. If not, we must revise it and repeat the process until satisfied. It takes time to get to a point of clarity. And the more complex a matter is, the more time it takes.

We should also not burden our writing with too much detail and too many legal caveats, especially not in commercial communication. Instead, we should think through what are the important details and only bring these out.

It is our duty to think through all of the legal nuances and guide our clients with as much plain clarity as possible. Such an approach forces us lawyers to think matters through deeply and only write down the most important points.

Sometimes when we work on a legal matter – say analyse a complex situation and try to find a solution – we may lose touch with reality. We get so interested in the intrigue of the matter, so fascinated by various ways of handling it, that we neglect to keep in mind what actually matters for our client – a clear answer.

What is not clear legal drafting?

Lawyers who send their clients long memos on complex legal topics are often not helping them because this means the client needs to do the heavy processing. The client needs to try and understand what is the essence of this memo because their lawyer did not present it to them in a manner that would be easy to understand.

Is it not funny that while clients pay us for legal advice, they still need to put in considerable effort in understanding what our advice is. We should be able to do better than that.

Clear and concise writing takes effort and requires time to put in the effort. Time, however, is something we are all very much lacking these days.

> *Speaking from experience, I have received legal advice that I had to spend hours trying to understand. Reading it back and forth. Taking breaks. Going over all of the pages several times. Trying hard to gather and decipher the knowledge hidden there. This has made me realise how uncomfortable our clients' shoes can sometimes be. Perhaps our clients do not want to disrespect us or embarrass*

Dealing with the written word

> *themselves, and therefore do not say anything. Whatever the reason, the circle keeps going – we provide them with complex legal opinions, they have to study them for hours, and then we try to have conversations around that. Is this really the best approach? Is this good client service?*

What actually helps clients?

When we put forward work to our clients, we often focus on outlining associated risks and consequences. We try hard to identify all relevant risks. And we offer solutions to mitigate such risks.

Eventually, it is the client who needs to make an informed decision based on the information they have received. But legal matters are often just a fraction of what our clients need to deal with in their respective businesses.

Therefore our legal opinion on any given matter can only go so far. Our client's management may be willing to take a risk that has been identified by us as a red flag. Because from their vantage point it makes sense to progress in business, regardless of the potential risks we have identified. This means that they see the risk as secondary given the wider picture they are working with. Now this may be shocking to some of us, but it happens more often than we would like to know as outside counsels.

While we are doing our best to advise our clients to steer away from all possible risks, the reality is that advancement in business comes with associated risks. Merely just being in business is risky. Not to even mention clients that are doing groundbreaking work (for example, in original assets).

As outside counsels we have the burden of providing a legal opinion while also having the comfort of not needing to make a decision and take action based on it. While this gives us freedom of thought, it does not force us to truly consider possible avenues of action. We are therefore one layer removed from reality, whereas it is our clients who inevitably have to deal with the reality.

If I happen to be wearing a client's shoes, I do my best to read the legal advice and draw conclusions from it for my particular matter. When I am not satisfied with where I arrive at, I will follow up with the outside counsel who delivered the advice. This is where I try to ask them 'what would they do if they were in my shoes'?

That question sometimes opens up the discussion from a whole new vantage point. Hopefully, the outside counsel is willing to put their red flag down for just a moment and think more holistically. This is how I often get the most helpful feel of the situation and the best advice. These are also the conversations that have the highest perceived value for me and pave a strong foundation to sustainable relationships.

As lawyers we have developed a superior risk sensitivity. We are able to look at a risk and quickly grade it as red, amber or green. We are able to consider the associated consequences and remedies. That is our true professional expertise. But that, in turn, may also make us resist change. Because with change inevitably comes risk. Our adversity to change makes us sit back and observe, rather than jump in with the latest advancements. But such an attitude may keep us from great achievements. It may keep us from learning the new tools that are available to us, and instead make us stay in the perceived comfort of the past.

4.2　HOW TO WRITE BETTER WITH AI TOOLS

Written legal documents have moved through an evolution in the recent decades. Most of us no longer start writing with a blank page, instead we use templates and prior precedents to get us going from a better starting point. Some firms have also developed automated templates, which means less manual work in changing all the details in a document. All of this is great, but it is child's play next to what AI tools can do for us in terms of legal drafting.

At the time of writing, a general AI tool (like ChatGPT) already writes better than an average lawyer in terms of clear and concise legal writing. And the models will only improve as more professional language engineers (lawyers) work with them. Please refer to **Appendix 2** for an overview of various AI tools suitable for refining our legal text (as available at the time of writing).

Indeed, AI seems to be pretty good at getting the Oxford comma right as well.

No more 'blank page block'

One of the typical issues that lawyers have is the 'blank page block'. This happens when you are asked to produce a legal document and you do

How to write better with AI tools

not know how to go about it. You first need to find a template or a prior precedent. It may not be easy, especially if you are new to the firm and do not know how to find prior documents efficiently. So you may need to browse around, or ask an older colleague. That is time spent on not actually writing the document.

AI tools that have been properly trained can entirely take away the 'blank page block', forever. Please refer to **Appendix 2** for an overview of some good AI tools for drafting legal documents. As an example, CoCounsel can give us the first draft of pretty much any legal agreement, and it will be reliably good because it has access to quality data and precedents.

A colleague that I interviewed for this book said that he mostly uses AI as a remedy against a blank page. He said that it is much easier for him to ask AI to start writing an email, than to start from scratch themselves. Somehow, it is easier to just chat with a chat box and ask it to do something in a casual manner, than to start writing a legal correspondence to a client with all the necessary salutations attached to it.

Having said all that, some senior colleagues actually enjoy starting with a blank page. But we have to take into account that they have probably produced the same type of legal documents for a decade or more, and therefore, for them this is a pleasant creative exercise as they have built up a confidence that they can produce the document from scratch.

But how time effective is that? I would think it is not effective at all, unless you do this just for the outline of the legal document and then go back to precedents and fill in this outline with the relevant content.

Cure for the 'template fallacy'

Another prevalent issue in drafting documents is the 'template fallacy'. Having a template in the first place, and using it for producing a new legal document, makes us blind to the potential shortcomings of such template. We have built up a false belief that everything is going to be fine if we use a good template. But as we review it, we may omit some of the circumstances of our current situation which may be quite different from the circumstances that were the basis for producing the template.

Having worked with a similar type of legal document for several years, we may do our best to look but we may simply not see. As we have seen the same words in the same sequence so many times prior. We do not even notice them anymore.

So we need to use checklists to cross-reference all the relevant circumstances that were used to build this template, to make sure our current situation is compatible, and change the template where necessary.

Therefore, while it is great to have templates, there are a variety of issues that come with using them. This is where AI can again save us from the trouble of working with templates and its potential pitfalls.

How does it work? Ideally, a well-trained AI has all the knowledge of your firm's good templates and good precedents. It has read them all. It knows them through and through, and can draw knowledge from them in seconds. (If your firm does not have a strong knowledge base, then you can use a model that has been trained on other quality data that is compatible with your practice area.)

That is all made easily accessible by using an interface where you can ask the AI to give you what you need. The same way as you would ask a colleague to help you out. And you are in full control of the outcome – you can review it and tweak it. So, you will have a much better starting point with an AI than trying to make use of a generic template or old precedent.

To some of the more seasoned colleagues it may feel like AI is yet another tool we need to learn and it will add to the ever-increasing complexity of our daily toolkit. While admittedly our tech stack has been ever increasing, I do hope that in the near term the AI interface will combine most of the tech at the back end, leaving us only to interact with our user-friendly AI interface and asking it for whatever we need across all technology.

Please refer to **Appendix 2** for AI tools that are able to work on top of your firm's templates.

Contracting, but better

Let us look deeper into how AI can help us produce a legal contract.

As an example, we can ask AI to produce an outline of a shareholders' agreement. We can say that we are representing a strategic investor who would be looking for all the customary investor protection terms. We can further note the relevant jurisdiction (if we have a compatible model) and any other instructions we have. And let the AI provide us with the first draft, in seconds. I have tried it out in my practice with CoCounsel based on English law.

Now that is a good start but it is only the beginning. We now need to scrutinise the first draft the same way we would scrutinise the first draft produced by a younger colleague (although, this draft would be better than any younger colleague would be able to produce because they do not have instant access to all of the model's data). Remember, at this stage we only asked for the outline, as it is easier for us to first check that all the basics are in place, and only once satisfied we can ask the model to fill in the relevant wording within the outline.

While using AI tools we still need to bring our legal expertise. Ultimately, we are still the ones responsible for the delivery in front of our clients. Therefore, we need to guide AI in the process of producing the draft we are looking for. And we should not lose our nerve if it makes a mistake. Because it will. The same way as a young colleague will. And the same way as we will sometimes make mistakes ourselves.

I see lawyers asking AI to produce complex legal documents, and then upon finding one mistake, they lose all confidence and stop using the model altogether. This is absurd. Would you fire a first-year associate after their first mistake?

A lot of this is perhaps due to not feeling comfortable with using new technologies. Because, after all, we are not engineers, we do not have a technical background. So why should we trust a 'machine'?

Well, we do not need to put our trust in the machine. We can keep it within ourselves, trusting our capabilities as lawyers. The machine is just a tool for us to use for the best possible outcome.

Please refer to **Appendix 2** for an overview of AI tools suitable for contracting needs of lawyers.

Infinite use cases for AI

While writing this book I interviewed some colleagues to see how they use AI in their legal work. One of them has taken their use of AI to a whole new level!

Lawyers as language engineers

He is a tech savvy partner at a London firm and he uses a variety of AI tools daily in his legal work. As an example, he uses AI for ideation and sparring ideas. When faced with a legal matter, he talks to an AI like he would talk to a colleague – brainstorming and exchanging ideas. AI is perfect for this. AI is also great for 'wargaming' where we try out arguments for two or more parties with different agendas. We can ask the AI to take the position of each party and try out a situation by essentially arguing with itself. That can be extremely helpful in negotiations with multiple stakeholders. You can also ask the model to play 'devil's advocate' for whatever argument you are putting forward and essentially tear it into pieces. That in turn helps you to improve your position.

AI tools are also great for analysing data and drawing conclusions from it for benchmarking or other purposes. Law firm partners often find themselves tasked with a variety of responsibilities that go well beyond purely legal matters. They may need to oversee budgets, they may need to hire people, etc. Many of these ancillary tasks to legal services greatly benefit from the use of AI tools.

Another good use of AI takes place in our work across practice areas where we may not be a specialist in. Every once in a while, we receive questions from our clients that fall outside of our area of expertise. If this happens, we may have the comfort of referring the question to another colleague within the firm, who is an expert in the field, or not. In the latter case, and if we still wish to help our client, we may need to do a bit of research into this new area ourselves. If we happen to have a specialist AI tool at hand, then this could be very valuable in bringing understanding to this new topic for us, and enable us to advise the client with their question.

> I know a lawyer who still to this date worries about a piece of legal advice they provided to a client many years ago. As it was outside of their expertise, they are still questioning whether it was the correct advice. It is important to note that the statute of limitations has long passed. But the lawyer is still worried. If they had had access to a specialist AI tool at the time, I believe they would have felt more reassured about their advice (and not carry this worry with them still today). Because the stakes are high in law, almost every lawyer has a story like that, keeping them awake at night.

Chapter 5

Lawyers as data processors

A significant part of being a lawyer is about legal research and analysis. From day to day we analyse collections of written information and draw conclusions from it. In a way lawyers are data processors in human form. We analyse legislation, court resolutions, documents in the data room. And then we draft summaries, due diligence findings, memorandums, etc.

5.1 CONDUCTING LEGAL ANALYSIS AND DRAFTING DOCUMENTS

We spend a considerable amount of time reviewing and analysing documents. This includes reading case files, reviewing contracts, preparing legal documents, and managing discovery in litigation. Document review, in particular, is a significant part of the workload for lawyers, especially in fields like mergers and acquisitions, compliance, and litigation.

Conducting legal research to support our argument or to understand a position is a very data-intensive task that lawyers frequently engage in. While importantly, data processing tasks can fall under both billable and non-billable hours (!).

How our brains work

Studies have been conducted of lawyers' brains and how they function. The primary focus of such studies has been on how the brain of a lawyer functions during decision-making, problem-solving, and handling complex information. Lawyers often show increased activity in areas of the brain associated with analytical thinking and logical reasoning. This is likely due to the nature of our work, which requires rigorous analysis and critical thinking.

Similarly to London taxi drivers, lawyers require extensive memory retention for statutes, case law, and procedural knowledge. While the hippocampus (involved in memory) may not show physical changes as in taxi drivers, there is evidence that lawyers have highly developed systems for encoding and retrieving complex information.

5.2 HOW TO ANALYSE AND DRAFT BETTER WITH AI TOOLS

I would propose that the way a lawyer's brain works is systematically quite similar to the way a language model works. Each of these maintain a collection of data and have different ways of accessing such data. In the case of a lawyer, we have years of accumulated legal knowledge stored away in our brains and organised through various connections. We can access this data by thinking about legal matters and asking the relevant questions. In the case of a language model, a similar storage and retrieval takes place (albeit much more structured and free from very human shortfalls like biases). Let us break it down further.

How language models work

Lawyers accumulate vast amounts of legal knowledge through education, experience, and continuous learning. This knowledge broadly includes legislation, case law, and legal principles. Language models are similarly trained on large datasets that include a wide variety of text, including all of the above. This training data is used to form patterns and relationships between words and concepts.

When faced with a legal question, lawyers retrieve relevant information from their memory. They recall past cases, legal rules and principles that apply to the current situation. Similarly, when prompted, AI tools retrieve and generate text based on patterns learned during training. They can produce relevant information by predicting the most likely response based on the input.

Lawyers present their knowledge through arguments, legal briefs, and advice. This involves structuring information logically, considering the audience, and adhering to legal norms and standards. Again similarly, language models generate coherent and contextually appropriate text based on prompts. The result is structured in a way that mimics human communication, whilst adhering to the context given in the instruction.

Using AI for transcribing meetings

Many of us already use AI tools for making notes. We use them on numerous back-to-back video meetings with our clients, colleagues and counterparties. There are various tools that work across commonly used meeting platforms. Such tools can make verbatim notes of who said

How to analyse and draft better with AI tools

what, thereby freeing up our attention to listen more attentively and to read the non-verbal cues of other participants (like their expression and body language). Please refer to **Appendix 2** for specific AI tools suitable for note taking. A good approach is usually to review and try out several tools and choose the one that works best for your specific needs. I have used Supernormal in my work for transcribing meetings and found it very helpful.

The tools can also give us the transcript in real time, so that we can easily refer back to it. Even more usefully, such tools can make summaries of meetings and collect action points for us. We can then keep such summaries for our purposes or share them with the relevant participants.

Some transcribing tools can even participate in a meeting during our absence and take notes. So in a way we can catch up with what other participants were talking about and read a quick summary afterwards – invaluable in today's fast paced business world.

With such transcribing tools come the relevant legal risks. For example, as lawyers we may be now held more accountable for things that we say. In the past we were mostly accountable for things that we put down in writing, and felt like we could speak more freely, especially when in person with our client. But now, with many meetings happening online, we are losing out on such more relaxed means of communication.

Video meetings and transcribing tools may naturally make us more cautious in our communication. We may even want to avoid transcribing tools altogether. But we can only avoid them so long as they are inevitably becoming a part of modern communication. Our clients are already using them with or without our knowledge, so it is out of our control and we need to adapt to this new reality.

Using AI for research

There are various AI tools for online research. The era of manual internet search is over (thankfully!). Today we can ask a simply worded question from an AI empowered search engine, it will go online for us, and come back with refined search results. It will summarise its reply to our question and link the relevant source materials to it. Some tools even grade source materials for credibility, popularity and other metrics. So, we can simply ask questions and get well-worded responses in seconds. We do not need to analyse pages of search results any more, we can simply review and

Lawyers as data processors

check what is put forward by AI. Please refer to **Appendix 2** for tools suitable for general and also legal research. I use Perplexity daily over a Google search on any topic. It is one of the main AI tools I use and is invaluable for desk research.

Let us look at an example from the daily work of a regulatory lawyer. As regulation is constantly evolving, it used to take hours to keep up with it – to first find the latest regulatory advancements and then to analyse the complex text for extracting knowledge from it. With the use of AI, getting up to speed with the latest regulation passed in the relevant practice area now takes seconds. All we need to do is ask for a suitable AI tool to search for the latest regulation and to summarise the relevant changes for us. Or we can feed in long-form legislation ourselves and ask it to summarise it. We can also ask the tool to find answers to our specific questions, etc.

Why spend hours reading 200 pages of the latest regulation if we can use AI and get a quick summary of the information that is relevant for us to digest. Why would anyone read the full text ever again?

That is significant time saved that we used to spend simply to keep up with the latest developments. We can now spend it where we can bring more value beyond reading information and extracting knowledge from it. We can use our expertise to bring forward ideas on how to implement this knowledge.

As I was interviewing for this book, I talked to a tech savvy lawyer working at a top law firm geared towards technology clients. Hopefully, his examples of a wide array of use cases for AI inspires the reader.

This particular lawyer uses AI tools for researching a new topic that lands on his desk. He uses AI to also create structure for his research and to create frameworks for understanding a particular new topic. He described his research approach as starting from the higher level and moving deeper in terms of understanding legal concepts.

As an early adopter of AI, he uses it as an extension of his capability and capacity. It is like his second brain. Listening to him it was clear to me that he is the embodiment of a new generation lawyer that is making the most out of AI.

He asks questions from AI, but also lets AI ask questions from him. The latter is useful when starting to work on a new matter and establishing the relevant facts of the matter. He may have some info, which he will give to

How to analyse and draft better with AI tools

the AI, but he will also reverse check and let the AI tell him if he should get more info from the client, before he goes deeper on a particular topic. So he is essentially talking to the AI like he would be talking to a client and vice versa. Another way he utilises AI is asking it to produce checklists for tackling various complex projects. And then he uses AI (Whimsical) to create visualisation from his text and put it forward as a graph to the client.

In his own words, 'working with AI is like working with another lawyer'. AI is a great sounding board and also makes grinding on a matter less lonesome.

In addition to legal concepts, AI can also be useful in understanding broader implications and commercial elements of a particular legal question. Law does not exist in a vacuum, therefore every matter that we work on is interrelated to other domains which we may not necessarily be experts in. This is where AI can be very handy in bringing in a wider perspective. Sometimes the best argument is practical, business-driven, and not necessarily legal at all.

Risks involved in using AI for research

There are of course risks involved in using AI for research. When it comes to legal research sometimes the devil is in the details. So, when we conduct legal research it is important we do not miss any relevant details. Or to put it another way, that we find the specific detail that helps our case.

Now, AI tools are built to deal with a lot of data. This is why they are so helpful – because they are able to go through a lot of information fast and provide us with their findings. However, AI may miss minor details that may not be very prevalent in a large collection of information. It may also not sense the intricate nuances behind the meaning of specific words used in legislation. Now, if you add to this a junior lawyer who does not have experience in the field – things can go wrong.

As we develop into senior lawyers, we accumulate years of experience and form helpful frameworks for getting to the right answer. It is bound to happen if we work within a particular legal field for long enough. I would even say that we develop a kind of a gut feeling. Having seen tens or even hundreds of similar situations, we already have a good feeling as to where to look for an answer (and potentially also what to look for as an answer). And we are often right as we have trained our gut to know the answer through many similar situations. So we have a well-developed and controlled gut feeling in these things.

Lawyers as data processors

Junior lawyers do not have that. Neither do AI tools. So if we ask a junior lawyer to use AI to get through a lot of info and try to find an answer, they may miss something important. That is why, even with all the tools available, it is still crucial for a more senior lawyer to look into the case materials.

Now that is not to say that junior lawyers should not use AI for legal research and analysis. They absolutely should. That is to say that a senior lawyer still needs to provide helpful instructions for the undertaking (where to look from) and other useful pointers (what to look for). And having received a draft answer, such a senior lawyer should also check it and cross-check the junior lawyer (or AI) who conducted the research.

Essentially, the way we approach legal research and analysis remains very much the same. We just add AI to the team. Thereby enabling us to achieve more, faster. But we should not omit adhering to our professional guardrails along the way.

Using AI for contract drafting

Various AI tools can track our text as we write it and suggest improvements to grammar and also wording. They can even suggest changes to our style of writing. They work as a kind of writing assistants or editors that constantly monitor and improve our text. They can write specific clauses for us, or vice versa, quickly explain what a poorly written clause in a contract means. In fact, when trained well they can do most of the writing for us. In seconds. Please refer to **Appendix 2** for AI tools suitable for contracting.

As I was interviewing for this book, I asked colleagues to share their success stories. I include one such story here as an example of how things 'used to be' and how they 'could be better' in the future.

> This particular success story concerns a significant carve-out transaction in the telecom sector that a colleague was working on day and night for several weeks with a small team of dedicated lawyers. I should probably add that it was one of the top city firms in London (where such work hours are pretty common, because 'the client is paying a lot and they expect a 24/7 service'). Also, it was a key client for their practice area. So the stakes were high throughout, both for the client, and also for the law firm and the team in question.

How to analyse and draft better with AI tools

As part of the carve-out this colleague and their team had to negotiate a long master agreement and its seven ancillary service agreements, each with a different counterparty. While all of the contract terms had to make sense across all drafts and therefore each change in one of the drafts had to be taken into account in all other drafts. And, of course, all agreements were negotiated simultaneously yet separately.

Now, you can imagine what a contracting headache this is. This means several lawyers negotiating, marking up and summarising changes across multiple long drafts with multiple counterparties. This is a lot of work. Admittedly, this is also the kind of work that only the top firms with sufficient talent are able to undertake within short turnaround times.

It was challenging, to say the least – managing several contract workstreams, managing the client, managing negotiations with various counterparties, all of this while also meeting short deadlines.

The colleague who oversaw this team effort as the managing associate said that while they pulled everything together, and it was a major success, it also came with a personal cost in terms of sleep deprivation and overall mental and physical health. As typical in such circumstances, while the carve-out was underway, there was little sleep to dream of for the project team. So, the pressure can get very real in such situations.

We, lawyers, tend to have stories like that. And we tend to bring these as examples of our biggest successes. More often than not, there is a lot of stress involved in our success stories. Could it be the level of stress endured that makes it feel like a success? For some reason, no lawyer ever said that their 'biggest professional success was completing an important transaction in a nice and steady flow of work with no major stress factors'.

After hearing about this success story, I asked the same colleague to reevaluate their past experience based on what they know now. I asked them whether the personal cost would have been less back then, if they would have had the tools that they have at their disposal today.

Their answer was – yes, indeed. Today, the bulk of drafting across multiple agreements can be handled by AI, thereby freeing up some of the team's attention from being deep in the drafts and chasing every word down manually. Instead, they would be able to concentrate on high-level tasks. They would be able to spend the majority of their time checking the work of AI, explaining the changes to the client (building relations) and putting their best face forward in the negotiations. Essentially, they would be able to concentrate their efforts on the tasks that matter the most.

Lawyers as data processors

Perhaps, they could even enjoy the process more. Or have a smaller team of lawyers on this project and utilise the surplus workforce on another assignment.

The enjoyment of legal work is often not prioritised or even totally overlooked. However, only when we are able to get enough enjoyment out of our work, are we willing to stay at it in the longer term.

Using AI for project management

Project management is another good use case for AI. Every recurring project can be broken down to its relevant parts. And such parts can be reverse engineered to create a process. Let us look at an example from a transaction lifecycle. Please refer to **Appendix 2** for AI tools used in case management.

A typical large transaction starts with vendor due diligence, which is followed by an auction process, which is in turn followed by the transaction itself. Each of these three main parts can be further broken down to parts. For example, a typical transaction consists of transaction documents which set the relevant conditions precedent, upon fulfilment of which we get to closing actions, and ultimately, we also deal with post-closing matters. That is a whole lot of process that gets repeated more or less each time a transaction comes in. A perfect situation for machine learning.

There is a lot of 'manual labour' around transactions. Yes, we utilise templates and precedents, but every time we still go through the motions of conducting due diligence, drafting and negotiating transaction documents, etc. While such motions will still remain, as there are risks in each of these steps that require professional oversight, we can expect much of the manual labour to be undertaken by AI tools. We can also expect such tools to guide us through the process of advising on a transaction.

So instead of keeping a checklist for every step of a transaction, and circulating it with the other side as necessary, we would be relying on AI to be the project administrator, while we use our expertise and strategic skills to steer the transaction in the right direction, negotiate with the counterparty and keep our client in the loop.

We will go deeper on due diligence later in the book and demonstrate a reimagined process thanks to AI. For example, Siso Diligence has a great product for due diligence projects.

How to analyse and draft better with AI tools

Using AI in litigation

As a fresh post-graduate, I was certain that I would become a litigation lawyer. I wanted to learn from the best and spend most of my time in court. That lasted until I went on a couple of trials and realised that I did not enjoy winning on the account of someone losing.

Having been inhouse for some years now, I have come to accept that litigation is an inevitable part of any business. We do our best to avoid it, we mitigate and mediate it, and try to get out of it with minimum impact on the business as fast as we can. But sometimes we may still find ourselves in the middle of it all. And then, we have to deal with it the best we can.

So I talked to some top litigation lawyers in the UK and the US to see what their expectations are for AI. How their day to day could get better with the use of newly available tools. Please refer to **Appendix 2** for AI tools useful in litigation.

One of the litigation lawyers I spoke to would like to use AI that would be trained on (i) all public filings with the court and (ii) the subsequent judgements relating to each such filing. By analysing such data, the model could effectively try and predict the success ratio of a contemplated filing even before it is filed with the court (and certainly before much work is done in drafting it).

That in turn would help advise clients who in litigation often ask what is the success ratio of a potential move. Instead of saying 50:50 or something more intelligent to the same effect, we could cite the predictability ratio produced by our model (and thereby also demonstrate how much value we are able to bring to the client by investing in and using such clever models).

Imagine this – you are a litigation lawyer at a top firm with lots of cases under its belt. A client comes to you for advice in a particular matter. You strategise with the client and as a result put forward two alternative options. Next to each of these options you also pull predictions from your firm-wide litigation model that has been trained on both publicly available and your own firm's data. That model would enable you to tell your client that *'the first alternative comes with a success prediction of 60.2% and the second alternative with a success prediction of 53.4%'* based on our proprietary litigation intelligence.

Lawyers as data processors

What kind of client would not be impressed by that? Even more so, that also helps lawyers in steering the client accordingly. While freeing us up from the ungrateful job of fortune tellers.

Another major use case for AI would be in compiling witness statements. The model could pull knowledge from the case file and make sure that all the relevant statements are sufficiently covered and included in the witness statement while it is being drafted. One witness statement alone could take hours of work and hundreds of pages to compile manually. Instead, the model could do most of the drafting for us, leaving human lawyers to cross-check and fine-tune the statement.

Now, going even further, a kind of 'litigation companion' model could continuously learn alongside the case team as the matter is progressing in court, while providing extra value throughout the matter's life cycle. For example, when the opponent files their documents with the court, we could feed these into the model (that already has the case files). We could then provide instructions to the model to find weaknesses in our opponent's case and bring forward relevant arguments to raise with the court.

We could also use a case-specific model to prepare for the witness examination, again by pulling from the case materials and also previous cases across the firm. Imagine that.

The use cases really are endless, all we need to do is open our minds and be a little creative (but of course not too creative because we are still lawyers after all).

Having said all that – this is not utopia but is already doable today with the tools that are available. I have come across models that have been built specifically for litigation workstreams. You should try them out if this is your bread and butter – if for no other reason than because your opposing counsel may be using it. Please refer to **Appendix 2** for litigation specific AI tools (there are many more out there).

Using AI in depositions and discovery

Here I would like to reflect on the life of a trial lawyer.

> Another litigation lawyer I spoke to used to practise as a product liability attorney in the US. He was handling cases against various large automobile manufacturers. So, he was often up against very well resourced

How to analyse and draft better with AI tools

behemoths. And day in and day out he was dealing with thousands of pages of depositions and discovery.

He brought an example of an expert deposition at cross-examination. As this colleague was representing the plaintiff, the defence attorney would bring forward a well-known expert who would then testify on the compliance of the product in question, whereas each expert deposition would be transcribed verbatim. And this particular expert had testified in previous similar cases. So there was a volume of data on the expert and every previous statement they had made. That is a very valuable data source in cross-examination.

The trial at court works very fast. As an attorney you need to be able to think on your feet. If the expert said something that is contrary to what the expert said before in another case, you need to know it. Immediately. Because this is a valuable source of information that enables you to examine the contradicting statements the expert may be making at trial, thereby undermining their testimony. But you need to be able to point to a certain previous hearing and exactly reference the words the expert was using back then.

This particular colleague (being an ingenious lawyer) had built his own database of expert depositions and also a search engine that quickly enabled him to find the relevant information. Today, however, such magic can work quickly like a superpower with the use of the right AI tools.

Another example this colleague brought was from discovery. In discovery the defence was asked to furnish the plaintiff's attorney with all the documents that related to the product in question and that may have relevance to the case. However, it was a standard practice for defence attorneys to send a truckload of discovery files to the plaintiff's office. He recalled receiving hundreds of printed documents. It was known as a 'document dump' and it enabled the defence to bury the potentially problematic pieces of information in between thousands of pages of filler.

With today's AI tools, we are able to upload the volume of information and ask AI to look for potential angles that could help our case. AI will not just search for keywords, but also take into account the context of our inquiry, therefore doing most of the heavy lifting on discovery. Such AI tools can also handle information in other languages, effectively taking care of the language barriers that used to exist (thereby also rendering sworn translators pretty much redundant in their previous function).

Please refer to **Appendix 2** for some litigation specific AI tools.

AI-powered dispute resolution

In order to better envision the future, it helps to bring parallels across various domains. Legal services are meant for servicing clients in all of their relevant sectors. Therefore, it makes sense to look across client sectors and notice new legal solutions.

Let us look at an example from retail – a large online sales platform is processing thousands of transactions every day and therefore inevitably receiving hundreds of customer complaints. Such a platform potentially has a good value proposition for AI-powered dispute resolution (as it is consistently dealing with repeat situations that are low risk and low value).

How would such an AI-powered dispute resolution look like in our platform example? First, it requires that we set out platform terms where users agree to settling disputes over purchases by such an AI dispute resolution venue. Then, the AI tool would be trained to tackle all of the more common complaints over purchase of goods (eg, delivered item is not the same as advertised item). Very much in the same way as we would train a customer support specialist to handle a customer complaint, with the difference that we only need to train one AI instead of a team of people.

Now, when a purchaser has a claim, it could turn to the AI dispute venue where they would be asked to provide their explanations and evidence. Appropriate questions would be then also directed to the seller by the dispute venue. Having collected the information, and assessed it under the rules, such an AI-powered dispute venue would deliver its resolution (by also providing the necessary explanations to bring the sense of 'justice having been made' into this).

Of course, the above solution comes with a heap of questions, like, how do we contest such an AI delivered resolution, is it even valid in legal terms? That is a secondary question however, as many businesses would be willing to take such risks of legal uncertainty, as long as it makes sense from a business perspective. So the primary question here would be – how much would it cost to train and run such an AI dispute resolution venue versus how much would it cost to continue in the old way with employing hundreds or thousands of people who do the same thing?

It is very likely that over time the AI cost would be much less. Such an approach could therefore be justified from a business perspective, even if we add an allocation for some future claims by disgruntled platform users into the risk assessment.

This type of risk-based thinking is how most businesses work. It would help if the private practice would also adopt it to a larger extent.

Chapter 6

Lawyers as therapists

When we work in private practice we deal with clients and their issues every day. They come to us seeking our counsel and support. Often they bring with them a legal matter that is critical to their business or to themselves personally.

The content of our legal service is only part of the equation. It is equally important how we deliver it. We need to take this into account when interacting with clients.

6.1　EMPATHY TOWARDS CLIENTS

A lawyer is often seen as someone who is unemotional, even cold. How did we become like that and is this even true?

As our clients often come to us in various levels of distress, we need to balance it out as professionals and remain calm in a stressful situation – which hopefully in turn calms our clients down as well, even if just enough to be able to discuss the legal matter at hand.

Some would say that we have become 'too calm'. On the one hand, it is a professional strength, but on the other hand, it may seem inhuman. Some clients may think that we are unsympathetic to their worries. So, in a way, our professionalism may have gone too far.

Having said that, it is often actually not true that lawyers do not have emotions. We do, we just keep them to ourselves. Because if we, too, become emotional then who is there to keep the situation under control?

Delivering difficult messages

Sometimes we need to deliver difficult messages to our clients. As you have surely heard before, 'how' a message is delivered is as important if not even more important than 'what' the message is.

Lawyers as therapists

We spend most of our career working on the 'what' – finding answers to questions for our clients. As a result of this, we have become extremely good at the 'what' part.

At the same time, how much do we ever contemplate the 'how'? Some of us may indeed also think of the best way of delivering a difficult message. But that does not feel like part of our work. Or does it?

Imagine this ... You have a client who is going to be hit by a tax bill and they need your advice to help them plan their taxes. For you, this is just another client. Whether they pay £100k more or less does not bring about any emotions in you. It is just a number. But for them, this may mean whether they can send their daughter to a top university or not. If you knew that, what would you do to soften the blow of your legal advice that says they are not eligible for the tax deduction they were hoping for?

The reality of our profession is that we deal with people. Even if we work for businesses, there are people steering these legal entities. Therefore, every message we deliver will be received by another human being. While they may not feel the pain personally, their personal KPIs (key performance indicators) may still be affected. They may lose their bonuses. And even if there is no consequence, they still need to likely deal with whatever we are recommending them. So they lose their time away from other projects, or from their family.

Working with the letter of the law may make us hardened and less prone to have human emotions. Because, after all, the black letter has no emotions – and thus making us also less attentive to other humans who we work for and with.

This is perhaps why an average lawyer is low on empathy – because we are not rewarded by showing any. We are mostly rewarded by finding the right answer and delivering it in a professional manner, whereas professional manners actually require us to leave our emotions aside.

Now imagine working in high-stakes situations all your career (eg, high-value transactions, or litigation). Often having to be the only one with a clear head during high-stress situations. This is how we train to put our emotions away, not to listen to them. But this also takes away from our empathy towards others.

It is a fine line between doing a good job as a lawyer and becoming an emotionless human robot. Some of the best lawyers know how to bring

Empathy towards clients

empathy into a client interaction. Essentially this is another way of building trust with the client – trying to relate to their situation and being considerate with our words.

Understanding the client's core issue

Another facet of typical client interaction is the lawyer's ability to absorb and dissolve client emotions. Clients sometimes bring their emotions with them. They can be generally stressed in their day to day and bring this stress into our interactions with them ... happens, all the time.

This is where a lawyer acts almost as a therapist – helping to understand and disentangle the emotions the client has.

This reminds me of a client I once had.

> This particular client was a very ambitious young investor. I came in at the point where he was not happy with the services delivered by the firm, also nor with any of the lawyers he had worked with, and certainly not with the fees. What an opportune moment!
>
> I tend to enjoy some challenges, but I especially enjoy situations which can be labelled as 'impossible'. Because this is where I have to switch out of my modus operandi and bend my mind around what is actually happening and how to problem-solve the situation. The best approach here seems to be the following.
>
> First, it helps to observe. Opening our eyes and ears and simply observing and taking in all of the information we can get. And asking questions. And doing a bit of background checking. Every good negotiator knows that information is everything. The more information we have, the better clarity we can find in any situation.
>
> As I was observing what had become a difficult situation for my firm, I realised something. I realised that no one had really shown respect to this particular client. He was young and extremely ambitious. And he was dealing with complicated legal matters that he had not faced before. No one had taken time to explain matters to him in a simple yet respectful manner.
>
> It may sound basic, but it helps to show our clients respect and understanding for their situation. To ask questions and listen to them. It is surprising how few lawyers actually listen.

Lawyers as therapists

> Essentially, this means getting out of our modus operandi of trying to impress the client with how smart we are.

> And guess what happened with this client after some open questions and a listening ear? He started to treat me with respect as well. He started to send me more work. He actually turned into quite a long-term client of the firm that I advised through many subsequent transactions. And he always paid the bills with no complaint. And I also made sure not to let my side down.

> This experience taught me not to forget the person on the receiving end of our services.

Personal cost to lawyers

Does good client service come at a personal cost? It does not have to. If we genuinely try to understand another human being, in most cases we find no malice. We will often simply find unmet needs.

Sometimes I hear lawyers saying 'I am at the mercy of my client'. This may indicate that work needs to be done on the relationship and communication with such a 'merciless' client. Because once the relationship is there, and communication flows appropriately, there will usually be mutual respect and understanding.

We do not need to bend ourselves to the liking of our clients. Instead we need to build relationships with them. There are many ways of doing that, and we have touched upon some in this book.

My general message is – if we do not like our clients, that may be our fault as much as theirs.

Lawyer mental health issues

Now, talking about lawyers as therapists we must also touch upon mental health issues faced by lawyers themselves. Some studies have concluded that around 50 per cent of lawyers feel stressed and overwhelmed. It is true that the intensity of our brain usage is on the verge of its limitations (although I would argue the more we train our brain, the better adjusted it becomes). Therefore, mental health is becoming increasingly topical in the legal profession.

Empathy towards clients

There have been various anonymous surveys of thousands of lawyers about the state of mental health in the legal profession. And the results have been very concerning indeed. Almost 50 per cent of lawyers feel that mental health and substance abuse are at 'crisis levels' in our field – that is one out of every two lawyers. Surveys illustrate that 70 per cent of lawyers are 'exhausted', 60 per cent 'have mental and physical overwhelm and fatigue', and 40 per cent feel 'helpless, trapped, and defeated'.

Another survey revealed that half of the lawyers feel stressed every day at work. Imagine what this does to your mental capabilities.

Over half of lawyers say that the push for leaner teams has impacted their mental health. 50 per cent of lawyers say they do not have enough staff and resources to get the job done, so they and their teams are stretched too thin.

From a business perspective, there is a direct and adverse link between high levels of negative stress and employees' productivity. Stress is often the cause of lower productivity, absenteeism and higher staff turnover. High levels of stress and a lack of resilience can lead to firm-wide tension creating a toxic environment, resulting in missed business opportunities, disgruntled clients and lost deals.

There are numerous potential sources of stress in the workplace that can slowly accumulate and lead to negativity: excessive workloads, lack of autonomy, misunderstandings and disagreements within the teams, poor communication, lack of work-life balance.

On any given day, we are faced by demands of our clients, colleagues and other participants in the legal system (eg, judges). At the same time, we are constantly dealing with the fear of making a mistake (every lawyer must tame and negotiate with this fear often), while dealing with the demands of our firm to bill more or our company to spend less.

There is this constant push and pull – to do more with less time and less cost. We all participate in this – lawyers, our clients and law firm managers. We are constantly looking for the best use of our brain and most efficient output in terms of value delivered versus cost.

No wonder that this brings about all kinds of mental health issues. There are too many lawyers who are constantly on the verge of burnout (and also many who have burned out and have left the profession, or thankfully got back on track).

Lawyers as therapists

It is important that we admit and talk about such issues and also that we take action, and ideally precautions.

High achieving lawyers are a bit like high achieving athletes. While with athletes it is perfectly normal to have a coach, lawyers do not necessarily think like that. Exercising our brains may be even more demanding than exercising our bodies. So, why not take the example of a high achieving athlete, and hire a coach as high achieving professionals, to be at solid long-term capacity.

A legal career is often for life for many of us. This means we would want to sustain our brains through decades of high-intensity work. If we start thinking from this perspective, and plan for say 40 years of productive work, it may become clearer that this requires measures to be implemented throughout such a long career for maximising our personal sustainability.

> *Having been practising law for more than a decade, and having managed with various levels of stress, I have personally leaned into a habit where I see a coach every other week. This keeps me in good mindshape and avoids burnout and other major disturbances. I have found it more sustainable to make the investment upfront than to pay a high cost of falling off the track. I remember being a young lawyer and hearing about a 40-something year old colleague getting a heart attack while on a holiday. And dying. Yes, dying of a heart attack on holiday at 40-something years old due to work stress leading up to that point. I could not believe it at the time. Only after living through some of the major high-stakes transactions and intensive work periods myself, I came to realise that this is indeed a very real risk if we do not take care of ourselves.*

Being constantly 'on'

Another major contributor to lawyers' declining mental health is being constantly 'on'. Almost like being at the mercy of the next client or partner, who can at any time put some work on your table and demand delivery within a short timeline. In a way, it is like working in an emergency response unit.

As a younger lawyer, you do not really have agency over setting your own tasks and deadlines. You pretty much have to take it as it comes, and find ways to manage the workload. Constantly juggling and prioritising. Attending to whoever screams louder at every given moment.

This daily stress builds up and starts to create anxiety. Anxiety about opening your mailbox to see what new cases are waiting for you today (all of them urgent, of course). Anxiety around how to say no or ask for more time, if you really cannot manage.

There is a lot of expectation at law firms about being a 'yes-man' and having a 'can-do' attitude. This is very much expected from most lawyers. But this means, in order to manage, lawyers need to have at least some level of agency and instructions in terms of prioritising their tasks. It is not possible to do everything at once.

A lot of tasks lead to a lot of multitasking, which in turn causes our brain to waste energy ... and so on.

We have to be responsive to clients and colleagues. And they have so many ways of sending us messages – on our computer, on our phones. At any given moment, someone may be chasing us for something. Now imagine, being in the middle of this, and trying to find time to actually concentrate on deep analytical thinking.

Which leads us to another issue – that is, switching between reaction mode and deep thinking mode. In reaction mode we are multitasking and reacting to messages. But then we also need to get the deep thinking in. So we need to take a moment, reduce our reactivity and get into thinking mode. Every time we do that it takes some effort. And as the day progresses it gets increasingly harder to switch between these modes.

Typical day in a lawyer's life

If I may, I would like to bring a personal example to illustrate the daily stress of a transaction lawyer.

> One of the 'highlights' of my career as a transaction lawyer was during the closing of a major deal. Our client was buying the target, for a lot of money.
>
> Now, closing is the final stage of a transaction, so you can imagine everyone having worked on it for many months leading up to this moment. Overall tiredness and fatigue, just the wish for everything to be over and done with.
>
> So we get to the crucial day of the closing, which we had prepared for with the precision of every minute. It was all ready to complete.

Lawyers as therapists

By 11:59 am the shares in the target company had to be transferred to my client because at 12 (noon) exactly the notice to the markets was due to go out.

But then something completely blew up. The share transfer simply did not happen. And even worse, suddenly I was not able to reach the bank clerk to get the status of the transfer either.

So everyone started to chase me. The seller's counsel. My client. My colleagues. The tension was building.

At some point I had a phone next to both of my ears – my client screaming into one of them, and the seller's counsel being supportively anxious by my other ear. While I was looking at my computer screen seeing new email messages coming every few seconds asking me for the status of transfer …

It was one of those moments where everything went haywire and everyone completely lost it.

Luckily, somehow I was able to sort out the share transfer through calm perseverance and sheer luck.

Now, this all happened within less than five minutes. You can imagine the level of stress hormones bumping into everyone involved.

But what followed for me? Well, as I said I had worked on this transaction for many months, through all of its phases. Every transaction lawyer knows that it is like a marathon with intermittent sprints.

However, stress adds up. Especially for the deal manager who needs to be the one keeping everything (and everyone) under control.

So even though I managed to successfully close a major transaction, the next day I could not get out of bed because of pain in my shoulders. In fact I could not get out of bed for a week. For days the only recourse I had was to roll over the edge of the bed, crawl to the bathroom, and lay under a stream of hot water until I was able to move myself just enough to eat something and get back to bed.

I am not special, many lawyers work like that every day. Even if it is not seen by their clients, sometimes not even their colleagues. It is only perhaps their family and friends that know how hard they actually work.

Steering client expectations

It can be challenging to be at the 'mercy' of the next client who may contact us at any given moment with yet another urgent matter. These days everything is urgent. And everyone is busy.

While there are exceptional circumstances when a high-stakes matter can indeed be urgent, often it tends to not be the case. On average, it is less than 10 per cent of occasions that something really requires urgent attention.

By having open discussions with our clients around delivery deadlines, we can also improve our workflow. We can steer client expectations in terms of our availability and internal resources by uncovering the actual situation on the client side.

It often helps to first clarify with the client what their expected time of delivery is and why. The why part is going to give us valuable insights. Sometimes we may be pleasantly surprised that the matter is not urgent at all, or what means urgent for the client is actually very manageable to us. As we ask this question, we may find an internal reason at the client which is dictating their expected time of delivery (eg, an upcoming board meeting). And here we could go one step deeper and see whether the client indeed needs the entire work product by that deadline or perhaps some preliminary advice or a partial delivery of the wider assignment would suffice.

The purpose of such a discovery is to understand where the client comes from with their sense of urgency. And to see how much of it really is coming from pressing necessity and how much of it is just their style of managing external service providers.

As we try to uncover and understand the client's situation, we may see that they extend the same understanding towards us. And if we then do our best to meet their pressing needs, they may appreciate our work even more.

Once we have a good relationship with the client, they may extend us the courtesy to take longer on some task or other. Ideally, it starts to work like any respectful partnership where both sides are dealing with calendars, deadlines and conflicting requests to their attention.

It also works for the benefit of our clients. If everything is urgent, then nothing is urgent. If the client always stresses urgency, then we get used to it, and after a while it may lose its intended stress factor. However,

Lawyers as therapists

if the client works with us at a mutually manageable pace, and then once in a blue moon something comes up that is indeed urgent, then they are sure to get our quick attention. Because, after all, they have not overused the emergency button. It is like a patient at the hospital calling for the nurse every minute. How many calls does it take for the nurse to stop coming?

6.2   HOW TO BE MORE EMPATHETIC WITH AI TOOLS

With the use of AI, we are able to send more considerate emails to our clients. As mentioned, the average lawyer is relatively low on empathy due to our training and day-to-day stress. We also tend not to be super communicators, simply because such a skill is not prioritised as part of our training. Some may say that we sometimes resemble more of a robot than a human being. While it is valuable on occasion, for example, in disputes where we want to remain level headed, it may also hinder us from building great relations with our clients.

Whereas if our client communication is sent through AI, it can add a nice empathetic layer to it thereby improving and retaining good client relations. That does not mean we need to leave aside our personable style of communication, it merely means we can get our message softened by adding a layer of consideration.

For us, in many ways it is just another client, whereas for our client, it may be a matter of grave distress and personal consequences. And we may not know about this at all. So why not be more considerate with AI, especially if we do not need to extend much effort in doing so. Please refer to **Appendix 2** for various AI tools that are good at getting the tone of our message just right.

Getting the tone of our message right

As noted, AI tools are capable of fine tuning the sentiment of a message. So, we can simply give them the context (ie, what is the message) and an instruction to soften its tone to make it more considerate.

Let us look at an example below where an AI (Chat GPT) is asked to provide a draft email in a sufficiently worded prompt. As a result, the AI presents us with the draft message which we can further improve and fine-tune to our liking.

How to be more empathetic with AI tools

Prompt:

I am a lawyer at a law firm. I have to deliver a message to our client saying that their position in an ongoing dispute is not strong legally and I do not see a high chance of success in filing a claim with the court. I think it would be more beneficial for the client to negotiate with the opposing side. I want to help the client in coming up with a strategy for hopefully finding a compromise solution with the opposing side. The client is currently full of fight and would likely not appreciate my opinion. Could you please help my message come across as supportive and considerate?

Result:

Dear [Client's Name],

I hope you are well despite the current challenges.

I wanted to share my current assessment of our position in the ongoing dispute with [Opponent's Name]. After a further review of the facts and applicable law, it appears that our legal standing in this matter is not as strong as was hoped. I understand that this may be disappointing to hear, especially given the unfairness of the situation. Please find our longer form legal assessment attached here.

I would like to convey that it is important to consider all possible avenues to achieve a favourable outcome. While the prospect of filing a claim with the court might not present the best odds of success, there is still a viable and potentially more fruitful path we can explore. Engaging in negotiations and aiming for a compromise with the opposing side could lead to a resolution that protects your interests without the uncertainties and expenses of litigation.

I suggest we strategise together to come up with a negotiation strategy with the other side. Rest assured, my team and I are fully committed to supporting you through this process and will work diligently to secure the best possible outcome.

Please let me know a convenient time for us to discuss this further and map out our next steps. We are here to support you and ensure we navigate this challenge together.

Kind regards,

[Your Name]

Lawyers as therapists

How does the above message come across? How would it make you feel if you were in the client's shoes? How much time and effort would it have taken for you to come up with a similar message from scratch?

Please note, the message does not contain any legal analysis, but instead contains a reference to analysis which will be attached to the message. This time we asked the AI tool to just help us with the tone of the message itself and not the analysis, which is not to say that we could not use the model for the analysis as well, as further covered in this book.

Getting our first reply out quickly

These days, everyone is online and messages move instantly. We have clients reaching out to us with their queries 24/7. It can be overwhelming, especially if we have a lot of work on our plate already.

Regardless of our circumstances, our clients do expect us to react quickly to their messages because everyone else is doing it. It is especially important if a client turns to us with an acute concern. This comes with a fair amount of worry for them, so they need us to take their worry away or at least quickly alleviate it to the extent we are able to.

It is hard to comprehend, until we end up in the client's shoes ourselves. Until we are faced with a matter we do not know how to deal with.

Imagine that you are buying your family a new home. You and your family have dreamt about it for a long time, you have found the perfect place and you are all imagining already living there. You are in the final stages of purchasing, packing your things and ready to move. But then something happens. Perhaps the bank withdraws their mortgage offer. Or the seller gets a higher offer and tries to back out. Imagine something that feels like a deal blocker happening to you and your family.

How would you feel? Most of us would feel immediately stressed. It may even feel like a matter of life and death at this moment. While our clients may not be in a situation like this, they may feel a similar level of stress and impatience when they turn to us.

When a client reaches out to us, simply confirming that we have received their email brings a lot of relief to them. It is great if we can also indicate when we would be available for them. Now that does not mean that we will solve their situation immediately, it simply means that we acknowledge it and are there for them.

How to be more empathetic with AI tools

Now the client can start planning for the discussions, getting all their facts in order and so forth. They have turned into a more proactive mode, whereas initially they were reactive. What made the difference? A professional that they need support from, has extended such support.

From the client's perspective, they have received confirmation that we are indeed alive, we have not gone on vacation and tuned out. It may sound very simplistic, but our clients often need this confirmation. Maybe they have dealt with lawyers who do not respond at all for days. Perhaps we ourselves have not always been very responsive. Therefore, they may be anxious and worried until we reply.

Such a first interaction is extremely important and it is necessary for it to take place promptly. Some firms have a standard to reply within a maximum of four business hours. That is reasonable in today's fast paced world. If our clients get no reply, they may become impatient and may start looking for another outside counsel. In any case, we have already let them down. Because we have left them hanging with their worry and no sign of life from us to be there for them.

Let us imagine how the use of AI could alleviate some of the pain around getting the first reply out to the client quickly.

AI first responder

Let us take an example of a medium-size firm with a wide client base and a number of lawyers working in specialist teams. Busy day to day, and lots of clients to service.

A law firm like that may decide to use an AI solution that sits on top of their lawyers' mailboxes and calendars. This AI would recognise when a suitable client request comes in and react to it promptly. It would be able to verify the client and their matter based on information in the firm's internal databases (CRM, DMS, etc).

Now, after identifying the client request and checking it against internal information, the AI could quickly send out the first reply. Such reply would not contain any legal advice, but would simply confirm that the request has been received, that the lawyer in question is indeed currently at work, and that the client's request would be processed at an indicated time when the lawyer is next available.

Such AI would pull information from the lawyer's calendar and also prioritise the urgency of the client request by analysing it for relevant signs.

Lawyers as therapists

Essentially, AI would take on the first line of response allowing the lawyer to continue their day according to their calendar, and inserting a new task for when there is an available time slot.

The client that reached out could get a pretty much instant response with the acknowledgement that their request has been received and will be looked into at a designated time. The client can now stop thinking about chasing the lawyer down, and instead start to look forward to the upcoming interaction or initial response from the lawyer, once the lawyer gets to their matter.

People generally tend to be accommodating if they know about the circumstances of their service provider. If we let our clients know how busy we are and when we can get back to them, we may see them being more accommodating to our needs as well. It is a matter of thoughtful communication that helps both sides.

That is a hypothetical solution that needs to be tested out to get to the right proposition. But it is already achievable with today's technology and could indeed greatly alleviate the first contact pain point for both sides.

Part III

New generation law firms

INTRODUCTION

It is inevitable that new technologies and new generations make their impact on how law firms are structured and how they provide legal services to their clients.

New technologies have brought us video meetings with our clients and colleagues all across the world, that many of us now enjoy (or not). Similarly, new generations have brought more flexible working conditions that many of us now enjoy (or not).

Likewise, AI tools are shaping how we work as lawyers, which is also shaping the structure of law firms as collectives of hard working lawyers.

As an example, a senior lawyer working on a complex transaction used to need quite a few lawyers on their team to do the heavy paper lifting – ie, to analyse data, draft documents and provide legal advice to the client. In the near future, a senior lawyer would be able to do most of their work by themselves or with the help of a tech savvy junior lawyer.

Similarly, we can expect less need for lawyers in inhouse teams. A general counsel with no direct reports is a very likely future outlook for some types of businesses (those with less administrative overhaul).

So, instead of junior lawyers, the senior lawyers will have increasingly more powerful AI tools at their disposal. They can get more work done than ever before, and have more space of mind to think about things that really matter for the client or the company they work for. This is made feasible thanks to the rapid development of various AI tools.

The need for less human power in delivering legal services inevitably leads to smaller law firm sizes. At the same time, it also leads to a higher number of firms because the entry threshold to the market becomes lower (less human power is required to run a competitive firm). Similarly, a solo legal practitioner can now deliver legal advice to many more clients on their own than ever before. They will not necessarily need several colleagues to work for them. They can get pretty far by themselves and with the use of AI.

Chapter 7

What does a new generation law firm look like?

We can see a shift to new generation law firms with like-minded partners coming together, doing great client outreach and offering quality working conditions to lawyers. Such 'new generation' partners may stand out themselves by putting their thoughts, values and personalities out there (eg, on LinkedIn). While doing this, they may directly position themselves against the Big Law and all of its notorious shortcomings (like 3,000+ hour annual billing targets, just to mention one).

Such public positioning attracts like-minded lawyers into their team, but also like-minded clients. Let us remember that many of our clients these days are inhouse lawyers and therefore often former private practice lawyers themselves. Having been through a similar training as us, and perhaps 'escaped' to the other side, some of them will have a sixth sense for their outside counsel. A new generation of general counsels will prefer to work with firms that tick all the boxes that are important to them (like humane work conditions, to name one).

> *As I have been on the client end now for a few years, I have certainly seen my sixth sense in action when it comes to choosing outside counsel. I am conscious about working with a firm that ticks the boxes that are important to me (a question that I tend to ask is 'would I work there myself'?). If the answer is yes, this means that I have approved of the firm's values, level of client service, lawyer work conditions and diversity. If the answer is no, then I will find another outside counsel. Because why should I give my business to a firm that does not meet my standards?*

7.1 PUTTING THE CLIENT BACK IN THE CENTRE

As always, a 'new way of work' will be a combination of (i) new ways mixed in with (ii) old ways that still serve us well. It would be preposterous to say that everything will change and nothing will remain the same. For example, one does hope that client meetings remain a part of legal service delivery in high-stakes situations – not just for the benefit of human clients, but also for the benefit of human lawyers too.

With the advancement of technology, something happened and we lost a bit of touch with each other. The covid-19 pandemic also played a significant role here. Similarly to the pandemic, AI will also have a groundshifting effect on how legal services are delivered.

When did you last meet a client at your office? We used to meet clients almost every day. They would travel or even fly over from another country. It used to be the norm before covid-19 came along – greet the client at the elevator, walk to the meeting room together, take their coffee order and sit down to discuss their legal matter.

But that is in the past now. The pandemic changed that. What was once an essential part of delivering legal services, simply is no longer.

Similarly, AI will have a significant impact on how we work as lawyers. It is already underway with the more tech savvy firms leading the way. And it is as inevitable as a pandemic.

We live at a time of AI pandemic and it is infecting the legal industry. And like covid-19, it brings along some benefits with it.

It is exciting to see new law firms emerging with entirely new mindsets – where the client is put back at the centre of professional services delivery, where the lawyers are taken good care of and supported in their long-term careers, and where the new technology takes care of the 'heavy paper lifting' thereby freeing the humans up to some extent to perform human tasks and have human interactions.

7.2 TALKING TO CLIENTS IN A WAY THAT SPEAKS TO THEM

As indicated, we live in the era of younger generations taking over from the previous generations of lawyers. With this also come new generation clients.

New generation clients tend to be more relationship and network oriented, and less impressed by the archaic accolades of a firm and the big numbers the firm has been able to pull in. Well, some new generation clients actually are not impressed at all (or may even have an adverse reaction).

New generation clients are looking for someone who is more like them – a younger person, yes, but also different in their approach to client management. The time of sitting on our pedestals and waiting for clients to come to us seeking our learned advice is simply over.

As professional service providers it is time to descend from our pedestals, mix and mingle among our new generation clients, and lean into their ways of doing business. This may mean connecting on social media. This may mean having interactions and perhaps even mutual interests outside of the legal case at hand. And mostly it means being genuine about who we are and what our intentions are. Perhaps it is the rapid technological advancement of the recent decades, but it seems like clients are more hungry than ever for human interaction.

7.3 BUILDING RELATIONSHIPS INSTEAD OF SELLING

Building sustainable long-term relationships with our clients starts with checking our intent before approaching them.

Every general counsel is constantly being sold to by all sorts of providers of different products and services. Relevant and irrelevant. With that comes the adverse reaction at being constantly sold to. And the suspicion that someone is just nice to you for two seconds, after which they immediately start selling whatever they are offering.

Therefore, the old ways of hard sales do not work on the new generation of clients. They are consistently busy, they have a myriad of opportunities to find 'what they need when they need it', and they do not really react positively to old fashioned sales attempts.

Therefore, new times call for more creativity. Us lawyers do not exercise our creative muscle nearly enough. Yet that muscle is there to help us find non-obvious solutions to complex legal questions. Similarly, that muscle can help us find new ways of connecting with our clients.

A good place to start is by observing our potential clients. By being more intentional about our relationships with them. And, in the first place, by finding relationships that have the potential to be a win-win for both sides. And then giving the chosen relationships the attention they deserve.

What does a new generation law firm look like?

It could be very useful for a private practice lawyer to determine their target client profile and observe where they are in the online and real world, who they 'hang out' with, and what that says about them and their interests. We need to meet our clients where they are and we need to approach them in a way that suits them. It is not rocket science, but it does require us to leave the archaic frameworks of business development behind and develop some new skills to tackle this new reality.

If we consciously find and build win-win relationships, all sides will win out of them. And we will not have to sell hard ever again. If we have made sure in the first place that the client needs something that we have (our services) and we need something that they have (their business), then this is the key to sustainability. It is up to us to make sure that we are the best match for the client. If we do not, sooner or later it will backfire.

It is very hard to squeeze water out of stone. It is effortless for the waves to carry each other on the sea.

Now having said all that, it can be challenging for lawyers while having all these sales targets and having to meet the deadlines. However, it does get easier if we put some time into rethinking our approach. Once we get the approach right, the sales get much easier. Eventually, they may even bring enjoyment because after all now we are surrounded by people whom we want to be surrounded by and who are genuinely interested in what we have to say (and sell).

7.4 BUILDING A PERSONAL BRAND

Building a firm's brand is no longer enough. It is the personal brand of a lawyer that attracts clients and also talent.

New generation lawyers have great communication and sales skills, without being too salesy. New generation law firms need to step aside with all their policies and encourage that. A big part of being a lawyer is about formulating and voicing our opinions. About advocating. Yet very few lawyers currently do that.

It starts with being public about things that interest us, and if it speaks to someone in our network – great. If not – great as well. This brings eyeballs onto our profile, which in turn promotes our services listed there. Because, ultimately we also need to make it clear that we have something that people may want to buy. What matters is 'how' we make it clear without being pushy or salesy.

Building a personal brand

The same applies to human interactions. It is a real challenge to be talking to someone and then see this person switching into their hardcore sales pitch. It is uncomfortable for both sides.

The lawyers who do client outreach the best, are the ones that put themselves out there, on social media. Yes, social media. We should not be surprised that social media has turned into a platform for legal sales, it was bound to happen. In fact, if anything it should have happened earlier. But well, law moves slowly and so do we.

Just look at some of the legal gurus on social media. How effortlessly they present themselves. How plausible they come across. How normal. A lot of thought and effort has gone into it, a lot of trying to 'find your voice', but once we do, it can become enjoyable.

> As an example, there is an M&A lawyer who posts something relevant and engaging on Twitter almost every day. And gets hundreds of inbound requests every few days. Yes, hundreds of inbound requests EVERY FEW DAYS. He has in fact left the Big Law and built his own law firm based on that reach. His account has had over 300 million hits in 2023.

A big issue to overcome is the fear of looking ridiculous. All humans have that. But especially lawyers. If we find ourselves sitting on a fence, what may help is to think 'what is the worst that can happen'? If the answer is 'nothing' or 'some people may get annoyed', it is worth taking our chances. Because only by doing it can we learn, improve, and master something.

It is abundantly more beneficial to sometimes risk coming across a bit annoying, than to not exist at all (on social media). In fact, at this stage of social media if you do not exist on LinkedIn or have a very bare bones profile there, you are likely missing out on social proof and therefore business opportunities.

Please refer to **Appendix 2** for various AI tools that are helpful in marketing and content creation.

7.5 SERVICING ALL CLIENT NEEDS

Just about a decade ago or more, the main clients for law firms were business owners and managers. As legislation has increased in complexity, and the clients have wanted to save some money on external

What does a new generation law firm look like?

legal fees, there has been an increasing flow of lawyers to inhouse positions. Now, the main clients for law firms are lawyers working inhouse. Often these lawyers come from private practice themselves. Therefore, we tend to get along – one lawyer buying the services of another lawyer where they need them.

In the future, we can expect outside counsel to be more embedded inhouse within an important client's business. Firms have been sending their lawyers on client secondments already for years. This trend will likely continue and may even increase. Alongside all sorts of interesting services, like a fractional general counsel supplied by a law firm to help the client set up or oversee their legal function.

The point of all of this is to be close to the client, to be where they are. To steer the ship with them while also on board. To be an extension of the client.

So, we can expect to see more and more firms, especially the bigger ones, to service their clients' needs in a more holistic manner. As an example, some firms are already providing executive advisory services to their clients. This service may be billed for or be presented as a value-add to the firm's loyal clients.

Through such advisory, the law firm is able to help the client's inhouse legal team on a much wider array of matters that they need to manage – from running the legal function to taking care of their stakeholders. The firm is thereby acting as a thought partner or even a confidant to the particular client. As inhouse work can be somewhat lonely, some clients will certainly appreciate having an external sounding board to challenge some of their thinking.

It is also likely that law firms will reshape into more fully rounded strategy and consultancy firms, thereby providing a heap of extra value alongside 'merely' legal work. The closer firms get to their clients, the more they can learn about their needs, and the better they can cater to such needs. It is also beneficial to the client if legal matters can be better embedded in their overall business and strategy.

7.6 TAKING CARE OF THE FIRM'S MAIN ASSET – LAWYERS

Needless, but somehow still necessary to say – without lawyers, we would not have any law firms, and we could not provide any services to clients.

All law firms need to keep up with technological innovation

The rapid increase of lawyer mental health issues is something that we all need to take seriously and that is therefore covered throughout this book.

Market forces work here as well – lawyers will go and work at a firm that meets their needs and requirements. The new generation law firm is a place where lawyers want to work. So, it is a commitment for both sides – the lawyer and the firm. And both sides need to fulfil their part of the bargain.

Further, in terms of taking good care of lawyers, during the past decade we have seen a significant increase in female partners and that is certainly something worth noticing. A new generation law firm is best built on equal opportunity, and is overall a better growing field for ambitious lawyers of all genders. Because, let us remember, half of all the lawyers are female.

At the firm level, if we do not make use of this potential, we are losing out on half of the opportunities – to win over clients, to bring in revenue, to service clients with quality legal advice, and thereby to grow the firm. Empowering female lawyers makes sense from a purely capitalist point of view.

> I prefer to work with younger lawyers. I do not care if they are a partner yet or not. I especially prefer to work with younger female attorneys. Why? Because, I used to be a young female attorney myself. I can relate to their journey, and why not give them a hand up if I can. I would rather use my legal budget to give a career opportunity to a talent who might be overlooked in the existing hierarchy.

7.7　ALL LAW FIRMS NEED TO KEEP UP WITH TECHNOLOGICAL INNOVATION

The speed of technological innovation seems ever increasing, and so does the speed of humans trusting and increasingly relying on various new solutions and systems. We have already given them access to a lot of our attention and daily activity, so it is fair to expect this trend to continue.

The overall technological innovation has brought an increase of tech savvy clients who may work at a technology company themselves, or who at least know how to use technology in their work. Such clients may be innovating their own business, and may expect their outside counsel to do the same (or at least to do the bare minimum).

What does a new generation law firm look like?

We could not imagine today that an outside counsel would refuse to send an email or refuse a video meeting, demanding a written letter or physical meeting instead. The same can be expected of AI tools – our clients will start asking us to be effective in our work delivery and use the available tools (especially if they themselves are using such tools to great effect). Therefore, we need to move to the level where our clients are, and this also concerns their use of technology.

Similarly, it is inevitable for younger generations to gradually take over from the previous generations. Anyone saying 'we have done this for 25 years and we are not going to change it now' is very much backwards. Trying to stick with the status quo is a losing mindset. Instead, we need to be agile and adaptive to change – because with change also come great opportunities.

Younger generations of lawyers have an 'unfair advantage' having grown up with an iPhone in their hands. They are much more tech savvy, some might even say tech native. It is easier for them to adopt new technology. They will master it faster than previous generations that did not grow up with such an advantage. We may even notice younger colleagues being much more fluid in their use of technology. They use it almost as an extension of their cognitive capabilities.

So in order to 'stay in the game', law firms need to be moving with the flow of technological innovation, as standing still means regression in today's fast paced world. And in order to move along, it could be helpful to involve their younger lawyers or at least observe them.

7.8 EVERY LAWYER NEEDS TO UNDERSTAND WEB 3

Let us pause here for a moment and appreciate the technological innovation that has been happening all around us over the past decades.

We started with Web 1 – looking things up on the internet (also called the 'read' web). This is where we learned to 'go online' and read text on various topics from all around the world, thereby expanding our knowledge base. We then moved into Web 2 – interacting with each other via online means (the 'read and write' web). This is where we set up a Facebook account and started to keep in touch with each other all across the world. And, we are currently in Web 3 – ownership of digital content and assets (the 'read, write and own' web). This deserves a closer look.

Web 1	Web 2	Web 3
Read	**Read & Write**	**Read & Write & Own**
Looking knowledge up online	Interacting with each other via online networks	Digital identity, ownership of digital content and digital assets

Web 3 represents the next generation of the Internet, brought about in the spirit of decentralisation, which in turn is enabled by blockchain technology. With the aim to address the limitations of Web 2, where data and power were centralised in the hands of a few large tech companies. Such centralisation of power inevitably brought a heap of issues – which tends to happen with too much control in the hands of those holding the power.

The key technological component of Web 3 is blockchain. Unlike Web 2, where data was stored on centralised servers, Web 3 leverages decentralised networks. This means that information and solutions are distributed across many participants, reducing reliance on single points of control (and therefore on centralised tech companies). (Blockchain also aims for interaction between different networks, allowing information exchange across various networks. All of which was not feasible in Web 2 due to control by centralised tech companies.)

But why is understanding blockchain important for lawyers? Because blockchain provides an entirely new way of transacting. It underpins many Web 3 solutions. Such solutions often leverage smart contracts and provide a wide array of services (eg, financial services built on blockchain technology, offering traditional banking services like lending, borrowing, and trading without intermediaries).

So, with blockchain come smart contracts. These are essentially self-executing contracts with the terms directly written into code (that alone should get every lawyer excited – a self-executing contract). Such coded contracts run on blockchain platforms and enable automated and so-called 'trustless' transactions. As you read this, just try and imagine how much work there is for lawyers to make sure that all of this is legally compliant.

With Web 3 come privacy and security concerns. Since a lot of valuable data will be processed via new means, specific protection mechanisms need

What does a new generation law firm look like?

to be in place. Added to this are decentralised identity solutions which aim to give users control over their personal data and digital identities, reducing dependency on centralised identity providers. Again, an important legal hurdle to consider.

It is important to also note blockchain tokens, which are used to facilitate and incentivise transactions within Web 3 ecosystems. Some tokens allow for unique digital assets representing ownership of a specific item or a piece of content (used in creative industries but also in real estate and other traditional asset classes). That in turn means all sorts of (intellectual) property considerations when it comes to digital assets.

Added to this, Web 3 participants are often structured as decentralised autonomous organisations (DAOs) – governed by smart contracts and blockchain, allowing for decentralised decision-making and governance. This raises many questions from a corporate law perspective.

So, Web 3 brings constant regulatory and compliance challenges – as the lawmakers are, like us lawyers, playing catch up with the innovation. So, it takes a seasoned lawyer to manage such a level of uncertainty for a business. This is why there is increasing demand for Web 3 related legal advice from the private practice. Such demand often surpasses supply as not many private practice lawyers are well versed in the 'new Internet' yet.

In fact, Web 3 innovation alone would already now sustain a team of lawyers at every full-service law firm, if they only knew how to tackle that. Like always, the more innovative firms are already picking up clients ahead of everyone else (who will inevitably have to learn and lean in as well, at some point).

By sufficiently understanding the scope and specifics of innovation in Web 3, lawyers can better grasp its transformative potential and its implications for various areas of law, helping them advise clients and shape policies in this emerging landscape.

It is only a matter of time when Web 3 technology and legal concepts will be embedded in many, many things around us, both online and offline.

Web 3 innovation will be further enhanced by the use of AI. One of the main issues AI tools currently have is centralised data (which means centralised power, but also centralised threat). Making use of blockchain would enable to decentralise the data and therefore take care of the current risks.

> *Web 3 is why I moved from transactions into technology. Because it is new, it tickles my brain. It also comes with a sense of mission – to build a better future for next generations. And I have not looked back since as it has provided me with new challenges and consistent learning opportunities. To put it in another way, I moved from Web 2 transactions (share purchase agreements) into Web 3 transactions (smart contracts). Therefore, I like to think of myself still as a transactional lawyer.*

7.9　NEW GENERATION LAW FIRMS ARE POWERED BY AI

Law is conservative, and lawyers are conservative, therefore law firms as collectives of lawyers are conservative too. Our clients generally want to take a conservative approach as well when it comes to legal risks (unless they are startups who like to 'move fast and are fine to break some things along the way').

Inside all this centuries-long conservatism, grow quite a few low hanging fruits. Like, for example, being nice to your associates and having a great environment for them to work in. By doing that you can win young lawyers over to your team and also ensure that they stay for longer. Or you could do better marketing and client outreach than the average law firm. Talking to prospective clients the way that really speaks to them, thereby winning new clients over.

The biggest competitive advantage in the technology era inevitably comes from being more tech savvy than the average dinosaur law firm. Firms that make use of the latest technology (and especially AI), simply will get more things done, faster. They can serve more clients with less human resources involved. And serve them better, cheaper.

As access to legal advice gets more and more commodified, lawyers need to find ways to deliver more services with less cost. Here a risk-based approach is in order. In lower risk tasks, much of the services can be delivered with the use of AI, while keeping the valuable human attention for high-risk tasks.

This is where legal tech companies come in. After more than a decade without much traction, legal tech has finally become sexy. There are very exciting startups and companies that have built products either for (i) direct end users (client-facing) or (ii) their service providers (lawyer-facing).

What does a new generation law firm look like?

We can expect basic legal advice to become much more accessible to end clients in due course. Much of legal knowledge that an average person needs is not a 'high-value/high-stakes' type of situation. Therefore, basic legal knowledge is perfect for companies to innovate on and provide client-facing solutions where people can rely on a chatbot instead of a lawyer.

After all, there is not that much difference already now in whether a client sends an email to the lawyer expecting a reply, or a client interacts with a chatbot expecting a reply – as long as the chatbot has been set up with the necessary knowledge and engineered to provide answers in a legally prudent manner. And is better than the average annoying chatbot. But if it gives free legal advice, customers may also be more willing to get on with it even if somewhat annoyingly.

Companies are also building products that are incredibly useful for lawyers as service providers. There is a mass of legal knowledge worldwide and it is already mostly digital (latest laws and regulations, practice guides, court resolutions, etc). That is a fertile field for AI tools.

Please refer to **Appendix 2** for a list of various AI tools suitable for legal work.

7.10   HOW TO WORK WITH AI AS A LAWYER

The way I work with AI is the same way as I would work with a young lawyer on my team. I ask it to help me out with whatever I am working on by giving it sufficient instructions. I ask it to draft contracts saying what kind of contract I need. And then I review the contract and ask it to make changes if something is not quite right. I ask it to do legal research, write up a memo on a specific topic, etc.

I ask AI for everything and anything I would ask from an actual human lawyer.

It has been life changing. I can achieve so much more, so much faster and with a higher level of confidence in terms of meeting all the needs of the business that are constantly coming at me.

Similarly, it is very useful for private practice lawyers in their day-to-day work. They can use it for all of the client matters they are working, on by of course ensuring that the model meets their specific needs and other confidentiality requirements (which are discussed later in this book).

> *Only us lawyers can and will ensure the soundness of our legal advice. Us, not the machine. We still need to be realistically rooted in our own capabilities as lawyers, even when working alongside a very potent machine.*

Chapter 8

Phases of AI adoption at law firms

Innovation does not happen overnight in the legal industry. Generally, technological innovation is adopted by lawyers within approximately ten years since the first early adopters. Law is a conservative field and therefore a prudent lawyer has never been seen rushing into making changes fast.

Therefore, it is realistic to expect that AI adoption will happen in phases over a longer period of time. Below is a general estimate on the adoption timeline, based on past observations. Needless to say, anyone who tries to predict the future is bound to fail at this impossible task. However, this should not prevent us from expecting change at the advent of the most potent technology the legal industry has ever seen.

Phases of AI adoption at law firms	
Shorter term	**Longer term**
• Initial staff reallocation	• New business model
• Ad hoc use of external AI tools across various workstreams	• Building proprietary AI models
• Training all staff in prompt engineering	• Emergence of AI assistants
• Hiring new staff based on their AI skills	• Restructured legal workflows
• Revising internal policies and fully integrating the use of external AI tools	• Reimagined law firm structure
	• Significant staff reallocation

8.1 SHORTER TERM CHANGES

Cost cutting is the most obvious thing that will happen in the short term. An AI tool can process infinitely more documents than a junior lawyer. And can do it incredibly fast. Therefore, it is inevitable that the bulk of data processing is going to be done by machines instead of humans.

Phases of AI adoption at law firms

Already now, lawyers are able to get so much more done with the use of AI. This in turn means that we do not have the same need for a team of lawyers around us. We used to working in groups, especially when it comes to transactional work. These groups will get smaller over time – much smaller indeed.

AI enhanced data rooms have been around for a decade already. And with the recent advancement of AI tools they are getting so good that they are becoming impossible to ignore. It is only a matter of time when our clients start demanding that we use AI tools in processing large volumes of data. Especially, in transactional work. And we better be ready for it.

In terms of contracting, legal work evolution has moved from using template documents -> to template automation -> to now using AI. We will look at each of these topics more closely.

Current status of legal review

Let us look at an example from the daily work of a transactional lawyer.

Every transaction generally starts with due diligence on the target (be it buy-side or sell-side). In large deals we used to need around five to ten lawyers per jurisdiction to review the data room materials for our client. And these lawyers had to have the relevant specialisations depending on the target company's business. So, we were each reading tens or even hundreds of documents and reporting any red flags that may have had an impact on the transaction or that needed to be reflected in the transaction documents.

Conducting due diligence is like working on a demanding project with multiple workstreams. It is a lot of project (and people) management. At every given time, as the deal manager, you are providing instructions, reviewing findings and chasing someone for their input. There is only so fast a human can go, especially when herding other humans.

> I vividly remember a large transaction that came in with a very short turnaround time. It was a competitive auction process for an attractive target in the energy sector. There were multiple bidders and my firm at the time was already advising one of them. So we had to set up a Chinese wall at the firm to be able to take on another bidder (after obtaining the relevant client consents, of course).

Shorter term changes

Now, we were stretched as some of our lawyers were already working for the other bidder. While we had to pull together an equally strong team for the new client. And it was all happening on a Friday afternoon with findings due by the close of business on Monday (of course).

My task therefore as the deal manager was to run up and down the floors of the firm and find suitable colleagues that could review hundreds of contracts in the data room very quickly. And be able to report back their findings by Monday. What a great proposition to sell to my colleagues!

The biggest bulk of the data room materials were commercial contracts. So I had to chase someone down with the right expertise. Luckily, I found a good reliable colleague who was up for the task. As a single guy, he had not much planned for the weekend and he was excited about the target's business. Here was my guy.

So, somehow the team came together, and somehow we did a good job on that. And our client ended up submitting the winning bid, which meant we could happily work on the transaction documents as well. And I am still to this day grateful to that guy on the second floor who was up for the task! It was a stressful hurdle to overcome at the time, due to the short deadline and necessity for human resources.

Improved legal review with the use of AI

Now, the advent of AI tools puts such situations in the past. Many data room providers already incorporate AI enhanced functions that help lawyers perform due diligence much more effectively. Please refer to **Appendix 2** for AI tools suited to case management (including due diligence).

There is also specialist project management software that takes it even further – by assisting in the task of finding the relevant information from the pool of documents, and also by helping the lawyer fully manage the entire project of conducting a due diligence. Such software enables us to have a view of the findings in real time, we can highlight potential deal breakers for further discussion with the client, and also process the finding by collecting conditions precedent and other relevant information for the transaction and beyond (eg, post-closing items). And this is all made accessible to lawyers, financial advisors and the client in real time.

Phases of AI adoption at law firms

With the proper use of AI in legal review, it will be possible to feed all of the hundreds or even thousands of documents into the specialist model trained to perform legal due diligence. We can then give the model precise instructions on what to look for and how to report findings back to us. It can do this for us within seconds, providing us with the draft report based on all the documents reviewed.

Having done that, we can double check the 'machine-generated' findings, review some of the source documents, and generally cross-reference the outcome of the model to check quality. This is where we would bring in our experience from past transactions and our knowledge of the target's business. Perhaps we would revise some of the recommended actions based on our knowledge of the contemplated transaction. Tweak the wording of the report here and there. And we are done.

The whole process would likely take us a few hours of enjoyable work. No chasing down colleagues. No instructing, reviewing, revising input from a whole armada of lawyers. Just a deal manager and the 'machine' performing quality legal review on a Friday afternoon.

The comparison is self-evident – a full weekend of around ten lawyers reading documents versus a few hours of the deal manager's time spent refining the findings put forward by an AI. It is only a matter of time until this becomes the new market standard for due diligence. At least in the big fat middle of the market (while there will likely still be high-end work for high-end lawyers and their well-funded clients). Having said that, it will of course bring a different kind of risk profile, which we will discuss shortly.

Fully utilising AI in legal review

AI tools will also work the other way around – they will help us to quickly analyse already existing due diligence reports. Let us look at an example from the future of a transaction lawyer.

Say we represent a buyer in a competitive auction process. And say prior to submitting their indicative bid, the buyer would only be able to review the sell-side due diligence report that is 300 pages long. And to make it even more exciting, let us say that our client came into this late and the indicative bids are due by tomorrow 5 pm. That is a high-stakes urgent situation. So we need to be able to assist the client in adequately assessing all possible legal risks, we need to be able to do it very quickly and without access to source documents.

Shorter term changes

In the above example, AI enhanced tools will enable us to review hundreds of pages of a sell-side report in seconds and bring out any relevant risks for us to consider and further process. In the process of using such an AI tool, we can specifically ask it to go and look for the relevant info. Here again we would be pulling from our expertise and thinking in terms of what risks should we be looking for? While AI will do the looking, and also put forward suggestions in dealing with each risk, it will be up to us to assess them in the context of the deal and discuss them with the client.

So yet again, we would be able to put more of our attention where it matters the most while moving much more quickly. We would be concentrating on the main questions – 'so what' and 'what next'? Meaning, why is this legal consideration important and what do we do with it? This is where our expertise has the highest value for our client.

The above is made possible by AI tools that know how to look for relevant data – where to look for it, and what to look for. Eventually, such a model will do a better job than a human lawyer would ever do (even with all the time in the world). But it is a matter of diligent training and protection against potential shortfalls. The model needs to essentially absorb all of the expertise we have as lawyers in conducting due diligence. Kind of like training the best ever associate of the best ever law firm. And this associate will never stop improving, thereby outperforming all human lawyers.

Such an AI tool can be further trained on the middle part of the legal review. It can be trained on what to do with each finding, and how to solve them. It will be able to assess whether each finding needs to go into transaction documents. It will be able to highlight potential deal breakers, again based on its prior training of thousands of due diligence processes conducted by human lawyers. Finally, it would be able to also highlight closing and post-closing actions, thereby assisting us in the full life-cycle of a transaction.

Human versus machine: risk profile

Now the above is an ideation and a simplification to an extent. However, we do already have the knowledge and the tools necessary to build such AI tools. So, it is only a matter of time.

It makes sense to develop such AI tools, because due diligence is a typical situation lawyers deal with, and it is a perfect situation for making use of AI. Thousands of lawyers across the world are conducting due diligence every day of the week. We all follow a similar process in doing that. The transaction standard has been very much globalised in the recent decades. With the help of appropriate AI tools, the human lawyers can work alongside AI and put their attention where it matters the most. Where any machine would fall short of human experience.

The above also requires that we let go of the current work standard where legal review is conducted by lawyers. What do I mean by that?

Well, work done by human lawyers comes with its usual risks. Human lawyers may miss information, may not interpret it in the correct way, etc. Many things can go wrong today, and sometimes they do. Let us remember that for cost saving purposes most of the legal review is already conducted by junior lawyers, who are more prone to miss things and make mistakes, simply because they have much less experience.

With the use of AI the due diligence process will not miraculously become risk free. The risk profile will simply be different. AI may also miss things, and may not interpret them in the correct way. Added to this we will have 'machine-specific' risks. Like, for example, coming up with something that is against common sense or legal principles. So, we need to essentially get adjusted to a different risk profile.

With the advancement of AI we will get to the point where the output of a machine is statistically better than the output of a human. We can bring a parallel with self-driving cars here. By now, self-driving cars have been statistically proven to be much safer than cars driven by humans.

With humans we have the risk of negligence and malicious intent, that is exercised around us by fellow humans. With machines we have other kinds of risks as machines do not have inherent intent. The important distinguishing factor here is in remediation. It takes a long time for a human being to change and adapt their behaviour. (We have also been known to repeat the same mistakes over again.) Whereas a machine can be programmed to take instant recourse, learn from its mistake and never to repeat the same mistakes.

Provided that the pace of the world continues to speed, and the volume of the data that comes with it continues to increase, we will inevitably need to start using AI to enable extra capacity as humans will naturally not be able to keep up.

Our clients are already relying on technology in their respective businesses. That is a trend that will only increase over time. So we can expect them to accept machine-related risks in due diligence as well. We can also expect to get to a stage where they would even prefer such new risks over familiar human related risks. Especially if the machine can produce results faster, cheaper and with less mistakes overall. Please note, this does not mean we will remove the human lawyer entirely from the process.

Current status of contracting

Let us look at another work example – contracting – a major part of any lawyer's daily work. Here again the AI tools can do most of the drafting and reviewing. Please refer to **Appendix 2** for specific AI tools suited to contracting.

A lot of our time is spent in contracting – preparing contract drafts, reviewing contracts, providing markups on contracts and negotiating their terms. We have developed templates to use in similar matters, we have applied automation where feasible, but we still need to do a lot of 'heavy paper lifting' ourselves. At every given second, there is a lawyer somewhere going over a contract, clause by clause. That is a lot of time and effort.

Our professional drive for perfection may act as a double-edged sword in contracting. On the one hand, we tend to go so deep in each term and consider every future eventuality. On the other hand, as we are so deep 'in the weeds', we may miss the bigger picture.

Contracting is mainly about thinking deeply at the arrangement at hand, considering its relevant conditions and risks, and then making sure these are covered in the contract in a clear and concise manner. That is hard to do when we are in the weeds. Bigger picture thinking requires us to stay above the weeds. Therefore, it concludes that the less we have to stay in the weeds, the more we can potentially think about what really matters.

Improved contracting with the use of AI

Let us say we need a shareholders' agreement (SHA). And as our client is an investor, we want it to be investor-friendly and therefore include all the relevant investor protection measures (right of first refusal, information rights, etc).

The other day, I asked a specialist AI tool to produce such an SHA for me. It was ready in seconds. And it was better than I would have made it.

Phases of AI adoption at law firms

I have probably seen hundreds of SHAs during my time as a lawyer so far. I have drafted and reviewed SHAs from some of the top firms, based on some of the best templates.

Still the AI tool did it better than I would have. Full stop.

All in all, this 'enhanced drafting' exercise took me around one hour. The clock went on when I took some time to write a thorough instruction (*prompt*) to the AI tool. And the clock went off when I finished a quick review of the draft document received from the model (*outcome*), having also made some changes and improvements here and there. All at an enjoyable pace.

It used to take me MANY HOURS to draft SHAs. I think the market average was easily around 10 billable hours of a senior lawyer's work for a proper first SHA draft. And that was just for the first draft, which of course would be added by a volume of work in negotiations that could easily go on for two to three rounds. Well, that is no longer the case.

What made my latest 'enhanced drafting' experience enjoyable compared to 'old fashioned' drafting is that I got to concentrate on a high-level view. I got to think through the important parts (what do I need from this SHA), while letting the 'machine' take care of the details (which I of course diligently reviewed and brought my professional assurance into, especially when it comes to nuances of each jurisdiction).

That is a completely next level drafting game, dear colleagues.

Human versus machine: numbers

The use of AI in legal work means less need for human labour. Which in turn means that savvy firms are able to cut costs spent on junior lawyers (who are currently doing most of the heavy lifting in high billable projects). Legal business is very human resource heavy and associates are a significant cost line for a firm, as we are used to having several associates per one senior associate/partner.

Let us try and put this in the context of money.

At the time of writing this book, one of the best AI tools specific to legal work costs around £26,000 per annum for a team of three lawyers (that is around £8,666 per lawyer). Whereas the salary of a recently qualified associate at a top City law firm is currently around £100,000–150,000 per annum.

So, to put it bluntly, If a lawyer costs £150,000 and an AI tool costs £8,000, then that means it is around 18 times cheaper to buy a licence to the AI tool than to on-boarding a new fresh-out-of-the-box lawyer. And that is before taking into account all of the added overhead for a human resource heavy business (taxes, continued training, vacations and sick leaves, etc).

Further, a core team of few senior lawyers can manage much more with the help of a specialist AI tool, than by simply adding more junior lawyers to the team. Newly qualified lawyers require a couple of years of law firm training to fully settle into their roles and become fully functioning and reliable team members. In the first few years they inevitably also present a burden to their senior colleagues who need to participate in training them and teaching them the law firm ropes. It is said that for the first two to three years the firm is investing in a new lawyer, and the benefits of such investment are reaped later on (by the firm or its competitor).

It is therefore obvious that in the short term firms will incorporate AI tools into their workflows and reduce their newly qualified intake.

This will bring up the inevitable question – how to bill the work that has been largely done by a machine? As we are used to billing lawyers' time on a matter, we now need to figure out how to bill the combined effort of a lawyer and a machine. More on that later in the book.

Other tactical responses by law firms

In the medium term there are tactical responses (eg, making sure that all staff are trained in prompt engineering). Certainly AI skills are very valuable in terms of new recruits as well.

Already today, lawyers all across the globe can produce more work and do it faster than ever before with the use of AI. So, it is obvious that law firms need to put in place internal policies for the use of such models by their lawyers. And train their staff to make the most out of such new tools.

In implementing internal policies around the use of AI, it is important to emphasise that the ultimate responsibility for the work product, and also for the ways the work product was obtained, still lies with the responsible lawyer. Nothing has changed in this respect (yet) – it is still us lawyers

Phases of AI adoption at law firms

providing legal advice to our clients and bringing our professional assurance into it.

Having said that, we need to more deeply consider the 'how' – how the work is produced with the use of an AI tool.

What kind of AI tool is useful for a lawyer

I will try to give some pointers on how to find a model that is best suited for your legal work. Please feel free to use these principles when assessing the suitability of AI tools in **Appendix 2** for your daily work as a lawyer.

The best AI tools for lawyers to work with are the ones that (1) have been *trained on quality data* that is suited for a specific lawyer's work, and preferably (2) trained or at least *quality controlled by practising lawyers* within the same specific field.

As an example, a lawyer practising corporate law in the UK, would want to work with a model that has been trained on the UK corporate legislation, practice guidelines and quality templates. And ideally such a model would also be (3) *extracting knowledge from the latest legislation* in real time. Exactly as a lawyer would check the latest laws and regulations to make sure their advice is current.

Now, the model also needs to (4) have the relevant programming to *mitigate some of the common issues that may occur*. As an example, the model needs to be instructed not to put forward an answer that is not based on facts. This takes care of the 'hallucination' issue that has been pointed out as critique on some generic models. It is therefore preferable for the model to say it does not know the answer (when it does not know it), instead of inventing (generating) one.

It is also necessary for a model to (5) *link its answers to the source data*. That is especially relevant in legal research. If we ask a question, we want an answer grounded in reality – exactly how a lawyer would present the outcome of their research, grounded in legal facts.

There are AI tools available that meet all of the above requirements. I use one that is well suited for my needs on a daily basis.

It is simply a matter of doing some research, trying out a few tools, and finding which one works for your specific needs and meets the necessary baseline requirements outlined above.

Shorter term changes

AI tool is fit for legal work, if it has been:
1. trained on quality data specific to relevant legal work;
2. quality controlled by lawyers practising in the same field;
3. connected to the latest legislation in real time;
4. programmed to mitigate some of the common issues that may occur; and
5. instructed to link its work product to the source data.

As the adoption of AI spreads within the legal industry, the models will also get better. The models have already vastly improved since the introduction of the more advanced GPT models in 2023 and 2024. Admittedly, the more we use the models, the better they will get, and the more we can make good use of them going forward.

What kind of AI tool is safe to use as lawyer

Here are some guidelines to follow for assessing which model is safe to use in private practice. Please note it is a simplification meant for the average reader that is not necessarily tech savvy.

First and foremost, an AI tool needs to come with a professional licence. This means that if a firm uses the model, all data that the firm inserts into the model and also receives back from the model should be fully kept confidential and not used by any parties outside of such firm for any purpose. Such data should also not be used for training the said model (unless it is used for training the model within the firm's licence with no benefit for the wider model and its other users).

This is quite a technical point, but absolutely crucial in retaining the confidentiality of client materials. So, therefore, making sure this guardrail is in place should be the number one priority. If this is not in place, the model should not be used, or could only be used by strictly guarding confidential data and not inserting it into the model.

Now that is easier said than done. A firm that intends to use a third-party AI tool should spend ample time looking into the terms and conditions of such a model and also performing technical analysis and tests. Such a decision should not be taken lightly, because a mistake here could have very dire consequences (imagine a competitor of your client using the same model and asking it questions about your client's confidential data that your lawyers have inserted into the model – sigh!).

A good approach in choosing which model to use should involve engagement from the heads of the relevant practice group (to assess professional suitability) and also engagement of IT experts (to assess technical guardrails). Further, if the firm has an operations manager or a chief operating officer, they should also be involved to seek to negotiate the relevant terms and pricing with the model provider.

How to implement the use of AI at law firms

The model should be thoroughly tested before it is released for wider use at the firm. Therefore, the use of AI tools requires a buy-in across the board – from IT department to IP practice team). And there may be conflicting interests among these stakeholders that need to be overcome during the adoption phase.

As an example, the firm's IT department may feel uncomfortable with this new technology that is provided by an external provider. They may have a variety of concerns around it (as they should) relating to privacy, confidentiality, reliability, etc. All of these need to be looked into and overcome in the process.

On the other hand, the firm may have an IP practice area that may in fact be protecting some of the firm's clients against AI tools and their use of clients' proprietary information in the training of such models. Again, this needs to be overcome by looking into the specific legal model the firm wants to use and making sure it has not been trained in a way that infringes someone's IP rights.

I am certain that there is not a single practice area at a law firm that would not benefit from the use of AI in their day-to-day work, but the shift towards that will inevitably take time.

Phases of implementation of AI at law firms

Let us get back to our example on due diligence and how AI tools can be incorporated here step by step over time.

In the near term, we will see individual tech savvy lawyers using AI alongside their daily work on due diligence. AI tools are extremely helpful in going through a heap of data in the virtual data room (VDR) and helping to find the relevant clauses, to summarise the data in the VDR, etc. While it is just individual lawyers doing that, with no firm-wide policy, then these lawyers can complete their work more effectively and reap the benefits personally.

Gradually, we could see a more widespread policy and acceptance of using AI tools in processing large quantities of data. We may see law firms start putting forward fee proposals for due diligence where the initial review is performed by an AI tool (and billed accordingly as relevant, eg at cost) and the secondary review is performed by human eyes (lawyers billing time). In this set up it is still up to the human lawyers to ensure the ultimate work product, albeit they get to achieve more and do it faster with the use of AI tools.

In the medium term, the use of AI in large projects like due diligence will open up the market to smaller firms as it is no longer necessary to employ a team of lawyers to go through huge volumes of data. The accessibility of AI tools makes due diligence so much more affordable and thereby more accessible to small to medium-sized enterprise (SME) law firms and their SME clients – in a way, being a true equaliser between larger and smaller law firms.

All of this can, however, only go so far as it is based on the age-old idea of how legal advice is delivered to a client by a lawyer. Let us expanse our future outlook even further.

8.2 LONGER TERM VIEW

In the longer term, we will hopefully see more strategic responses by law firms when it comes to AI. One of the main strategic directions could be training their own proprietary AI on the firm's data.

Such an approach would have a high-value proposition to clients – a model that has the collective knowledge of all the lawyers that ever worked at the firm and all the documents and information the firm has ever processed.

Law firms will become redefined by their use of AI – the services they provide to clients and how they provide them. Firms that saw this coming and made the investment early on will have the advantage in the marketplace.

Phases of AI adoption at law firms

Phases of AI adoption at law firms
Longer term
• Building inhouse proprietary AI models
• Emergence of AI assistants
• Restructured legal workflows
• Reimagined law firm structure
• New business model
• Significant staff reallocation

Training a law firm AI

It is time for law firms to ride the 'AI wave' and get the most out of technological innovation that is happening all around us with ever increasing speed. Law firms (especially the big firms with lots of data) should start training their proprietary AI tools.

There are of course confidentiality concerns around using client data when developing a firm's proprietary AI. Client work may include confidential business information and such work product generally belongs to the client who has paid for it. Therefore, the firm would need the client's consent for training a model on their data. This could be solved by adding a consent into the engagement letter. Most clients should be fine with such use of data if well managed, as long as it is aggregated and part of a larger data pool, thereby making it impossible to use it for specific means (like for advising the said client's competitor). And as long as client benefits too.

In any case, such cross-use already happens within a firm – unless something is specifically guarded by a 'Chinese Wall', most data that a firm collects is accessible across the firm for lawyers to pull knowledge from. It is just happening largely manually still. As an example, let us say a partner gives a specific drafting assignment to an associate. Often the partner would also note some of the previous cases that are similar to the current one. The associate would then look up these previous cases, and draw knowledge and precedents from them. This gives the associate a starting point in drafting the requested document for the new client.

Firms rely on previous precedents when advising new clients on a similar matter. The bigger the firm, the more they have previous knowledge that they can pull from (of course, on a confidential basis and without infringing their clients' proprietary rights).

Longer term view

Similarly, a firm's data could be used to build a more intelligent model, as long as the firm would not use this data to build a model that would then be monetised on the open market. This is the line that we need to be mindful of – client data could be used for servicing clients better, but generally not used to build extra revenue outside of servicing clients (unless economics are shared somehow).

Training proprietary AI is essentially like training an associate that all of the firm's lawyers can use infinitely. One that will never leave the firm, never stop improving, never get sick etc. Let us look at that more closely as a step-by step approach based on what is available during writing of this book.

> *When I worked at a firm that had great knowledge management tools, if I were to open a new case with a specific practice area under a client, it would automatically direct me towards similar cases in the document management system (DMS) for me to look up and draw knowledge from. Such recycling of knowledge enabled the firm to produce work much faster (and often better) in the fast-paced service delivery environment.*

Approach to training an AI

The approach to training a law firm's proprietary AI is essentially three-fold: (1) assessing the quality of the data pool, (2) finding a suitable technical solution to use, and (3) building a bridge between the data pool and the technical solution for the best outcome. Let us look at these steps more closely. Again, please note that the below is a grave simplification meant to merely introduce the concept and not a comprehensive roadmap.

STEP 1	→	STEP 2	→	STEP 3
Assess the quality of the data pool		Find a suitable technical solution		Bridge the data pool with the technical solution

(1) Law firm data pool

When it comes to data pools, in the digital era, most of the information that a law firm processes is already digital. And the bigger the firm, the more there is – memos, contracts, emails, notes. All the variations of a single

Phases of AI adoption at law firms

contract with track changes attached to each draft version. All the emails on the same contract with the client and counterparty.

Most firms also use a document management system – DMS – with the more tech savvy firms already making sure that all case materials and communication is properly and automatically filed under a single folder. This means that if we need to access data on a particular Case X, we can find all of it in its designated space (at least we should, if the processes and lawyers work as intended which admittedly may not always be the case).

All of this is to say that firms have a lot of valuable information stored digitally throughout the years by its lawyers. This is seen as the collective brain of the firm. And it is extremely valuable (if we can easily access all this data stored all over the firm).

The bigger the firm, the more data there is. But how do we easily get a hold of, and even more importantly, make good use of all this data?

(2) Suitable technical solution

This is where AI tools come into play. GPT, or *'Generative Pre-trained Transformer'*, is essentially a technological solution that helps to quickly access and analyse data, and present an answer based on its pre-trained rules of getting to an answer.

Now imagine using such a capable and sufficiently pre-trained GPT on the volume of the information your firm has.

Instead of going down the rabbit holes of the DMS to find a single document, or running around the firm looking for an older colleague who could point you towards the right precedent – you could simply open a chat box on your computer and ask it questions like you would ask from another human being – in plain language. This chat box would in turn be attached to the entirety of the firm's data and it would do all of the heavy work of scouring through it and present you with an answer or a first draft (depending on what you were asking for). And do it all within seconds!

It would be very difficult to argue that such a tool would not be useful for law firm lawyers in their day-to-day work. Provided that it has been set up properly and provided that there are necessary guardrails in place in terms of getting to a good enough work product.

Longer term view

Please notice the use of qualifying words here – 'good enough' work product. This needs to be emphasised. We should not expect technology to immediately provide us with the best possible work product without any human interference. That is an unrealistic expectation and we as an industry need to adjust our expectations towards technology accordingly. Is it not strange that yesterday we had nothing, and today we expect the tools to be perfect? (And if they fail at that impossible task, we may refuse to use them.) We need more of a balanced approach. We do not expect a first year associate to immediately produce impeccable quality legal work. We should also not expect technology to achieve that during its first years of work. The tools will get better as we keep using them.

(3) Bridge between data pool and technical solution

This is a difficult step and also one that requires significant resources. Before we get into this, we need to acknowledge that the technology stack and therefore also the technology cost is going to significantly increase in the coming years for law firms.

The main cost line for law firms is currently human resources. So in the process of replacing some of its human resource needs with technology, a significant part of the cost also moves from humans to machines. This is inevitable and better acknowledged earlier during budgeting, than taken by surprise later on.

To bring an example, with the currently available resources, a firm could likely spend several hundred thousand US dollars on building their proprietary AI. That is money spent outright to get the model going. That will of course be added by on-going maintenance fees and resources spent on further improvements as the underlying technology advances.

Over time, the technology cost will go down as such tailor-made services become more readily available. And the investment in technology will provide the firm infinite returns over time.

Having said that, the key to building an inhouse proprietary AI is to bridge the right technological solution with the data pool the firm has. This could mean taking an external GPT and training it to work on the firm's data.

That is an important task that requires time, attention and careful management. This includes prompt engineering, checking against typical shortfalls (like hallucinations), and all of this. Expert advice needs to be

Phases of AI adoption at law firms

sought to figure this out. At the current stage this is very much a hands-on exercise where a firm needs to work together with a technology provider to build this bridge in a suitable and sustainable way.

It is worth mentioning that even with the best quality internal data pool, the model also needs to be trained on external data and its general understanding of the law. In order for the model to work appropriately it needs the general framework of law and how to approach legal matters. Therefore, some pre-training is required otherwise we may end up with a search engine as opposed to a fully rounded legal AI tool. A fully functioning model is like a fully functioning lawyer – it has the knowledge from general to specific. Therefore, we cannot omit the general frameworks from its training. And since law firms mostly deal with complex legal situations, pre-training of the model would be required before it can properly dive into the firm's data pool in search of the right answers.

It will take time (months, if not more), but it will be worth the investment in time and money.

Imagine the headlines:

XYZ Law Firm, 'your trusted advisor enhanced by firm-wide intelligence'

or

XYZ Law Firm, 'helping clients succeed by providing the best lawyers with the latest technology'

or

XYZ Law Firm, 'the premier provider of legal services, enhanced by human and machine intelligence'

or simply

XYZ Law Firm, 'go further faster with us'

This is the ultimate marketing line for the current decade in private practice. And a well-deserved one for those firms that have taken the leap and made the investment. It has never been a more exciting time to be a lawyer. (And a more challenging time to be a managing partner.)

As a counterargument to training the firm's model, some firms may take an approach to use a variety of external models and integrate them with their internal data. There is nothing wrong in doing that. It is certainly good to make use of all available tools (while making sure they are safe to use in professional services, as touched upon). However, having a wide array of external tools does pose the question of reliability on external providers. It also means that the complexity of our daily work increases in terms of an even wider range of tools we need to master in order to deliver services, and they all look different! One can only imagine what extra pressure this puts on lawyer's cognitive capabilities.

Building custom AI solutions for clients

Similarly to building models to serve the firm's needs, more advantageous firms will start building models to serve their clients' specific needs. In fact, some top law firms are already doing that. Those with more resources are taking a proactive approach to AI, instead of simply being reactive.

In many ways, the advent of AI enables firms to rethink their service offering to their clients. It is one thing to use AI for productivity and specific needs, but it is a whole new level to take a step back and think in higher terms – how could we fundamentally change our industry and thereby also our business model? The latter approach takes creativity and a deep understanding of both the legal industry and technology.

Throughout this book we have touched upon various issues within our industry. From failing to meet client expectations to declining lawyer mental health. Why not take us to a whole new level with the use of ever potent AI? Indeed, we are only limited by our imagination and courage.

One of the brilliant colleagues I spoke to in preparation for this book, brought an example of a very advantageous AI tool developed by her firm. In particular, her firm has analysed a volume of data on cyber security incidents. In the process of doing this, they also mapped down what are the relevant required actions for a company under cyber attack. Such actions consist of various reporting requirements to regulators in different jurisdictions, and also notice requirements to different types of customers. Essentially, this firm took a typical cyber security incident into its relevant pieces and mapped it down. After having done that, they built an AI solution that is able to quickly analyse a new incident and within seconds propose a course of action by the company that is under attack.

Phases of AI adoption at law firms

The above constitutes an incredible value proposition to clients. It is extremely unsettling to be made aware of a cyber security issue and then having to quickly investigate it while also having near immediate requirements to report the issue to the relevant regulator and inform the relevant customers. It is a very high-stress situation and has the potential to paralyse the client organisation for the duration of the internal investigation. And usually it takes about a week for a team of lawyers to work out how serious the situation is and to come up with a course of action together with the client. That means a week of agony not knowing where the company that was under attack will end up. However, with the use of the said AI solution, a preliminary assessment is near immediate. And that quickly brings a baseline understanding of how bad the situation potentially is. And enables the lawyers and the client to work on the best strategy for solving the situation. Note the difference – a week spent on first uncovering and then handling the situation versus hours spent on assessing and strategising a solution.

We can expect clients to pay good money for bringing such quick clarity into a very uncomfortable situation. And if a client is in a high-risk category for cyber attacks, we may even expect them to pay the firm a retainer just to have this solution available. In any case, it is likely that clients will see a similar value if not more in this improved service, compared to the past level of service.

AI assistant as the 'first responder'

Let us look into some more imaginative future solutions now.

We are all familiar with online chatbots that have infiltrated customer support in retail, thereby replacing human beings at most vendors. These chatbots have proven to be somewhat annoying and often ineffective; however, we have gotten used to them regardless (as the alternative – human support – has been gradually phased out).

With the addition of capable and specifically trained AI tools, such chatbots can achieve much more in terms of actually supporting customers. So it is only a matter of time until the retail customer support gets much better.

Let us see how such AI enhanced chatbots could be effectively used in private practice.

With the use of a chatbot (let us call it an 'AI assistant'), law firms could be more efficient in handling their first interactions with clients.

Longer term view

When a client approaches the firm, a lawyer that receives the request usually has a first meeting with them. The purpose of this meeting is to learn about the client's details, perform a conflict of interest check (CoI), and ultimately assign the right lawyer to the client depending on the client's needs.

Instead of the above, the firm could use a specifically trained AI assistant as the first responder if a client turns to the firm. Such an AI assistant could collect and check client data against the firm's client relationship management (CRM) database to verify any prior engagements and potential CoI. (Should a CoI arise during initial discovery, a relevant specialist at the firm could intervene and seek to solve it.)

Such an AI assistant could further collect the relevant details on the legal matter by asking a list of questions from the client. At the same time, the AI assistant can verify the collected details against the specialisation and availability of lawyers working at the firm – and ultimately find the best possible, available lawyer to this client.

So, once the client reaches their designated lawyer, this lawyer already has the client info and a matter brief, and any CoI has already been cleared, thereby enabling the parties to dive right into service delivery.

One may argue that such a first client meeting is also an important touch point with the client to sell the firm's services and win the client over. That is a valid argument indeed. However, once the market moves towards fully utilising what AI tools have to offer, the first client meetings would take place after the details have been collected and checked, and the client has been passed on to the relevant lawyer. Thereby potentially making a better match with a lawyer who has the right expertise and also near term availability to present their services to the client in the most effective manner, and thereby have a higher chance of winning them over.

The logic behind the advance of AI assistants is the same as the overall logic behind this book – the tasks that require lower intelligence and are more repetitive, will gradually be performed by AI. The same way such tasks are often no longer performed by lawyers but instead currently performed by their human assistants. It is just another step in the inevitable evolution of using technology where it makes most sense, and equally spending our valuable brainpower where it makes most sense.

As the task of collecting client and matter details and performing CoI checks takes quite a bit of administrative time, we can expect such tasks to

Phases of AI adoption at law firms

be performed with the help of AI in the longer term. Even if it lacks some of the personal touch and our clients may not appreciate it at first, they will get used to it the same way we have had to get used to the chatbot customer support in retail.

AI assistant workflow
1. Notice incoming new client request
2. Check client data against CRM
3. Perform CoI checks
4. Specify the legal matter
5. Assign appropriate and available lawyer

Having said all that, there will always be space for premium firms that provide white shoe service. As a client, you get what you pay for. If you are paying high fees, you will get a VIP service. Therefore, the above example of AI assistants is directed to the (large) middle part of the market.

Pushing work on someone versus pulling work for yourself

Let us take it even further from AI assistants. Let us see what else could be implemented in conjunction with AI assistants as the first responders.

First, let us imagine a system where all new cases are collected into an internal pool of available work. The cases would be sent to this pool after having been processed by the AI assistant as per above. Meaning these cases would be verified and 'ready to go'.

This pool of new cases would then be made available for all lawyers in real time, and they could 'pull work' from it. This would enable lawyers to choose what they would like to work on, or the client they would like to get closer to.

Such a 'pull work' system could replace the 'push work' type of system we have been mostly using so far – where a lawyer is simply given work to do by their more senior colleagues, while having very little authority to choose or say 'no'.

Why not let lawyers choose what they want to work on and what kind of timeline they are able to deliver on? Everyone is anyway incentivised by various targets, so having such an option to choose would simply add a layer of autonomy and ownership to the work we will inevitably be doing. This deserves a closer look.

That in turn could help alleviate one of the most prevalent issues within private practice – mental health issues discussed in this book.

Issues with pushing work on someone

There is a major issue within private practice lawyers who have too much work to fit into their working (or even waking) hours. That has been the case for at least the last ten years, if not more. Somehow, as an industry, we have not managed to sort this out.

I would like to put forward a hypothesis that this work overload is largely due to having no or very little control over the work that we take up.

For a typical associate at a big firm, the work just keeps coming at them. From their partner, from other partners, from senior associates, etc. And they have to cram everything into their waking hours, because to say 'no' is a taboo, as we all know too well. Oh, and of course they have no control over the deadlines that have been promised to the clients by their more senior colleagues.

And as they are forced to take up more work, with each additional task, the admin overhaul also increases.

Say an associate is working on three matters for different clients, and has planned their days carefully to complete all assignments by their given deadlines. Now, say three more matters are added to their plate. This means that they have to spend extra time organising their days to be able to serve all these competing needs. Therefore, this means more time spent on admin.

And we have all felt first hand, the significant attention cost spent when we jump from one matter to the other. Therefore, if an associate works on six cases at once, a lot of their brain power goes towards admin and handling the case flow. Whereas if they work on fewer cases, more of their brain power is available to go towards actually thinking about their cases and figuring out important legal questions.

With an overload of too many cases, an associate may soon find themselves in a reactive mode – just trying to manage all competing needs, correspondence and meetings, while having very little or no time for deep thinking (apart from nighttime perhaps when the hustle cools down).

Phases of AI adoption at law firms

This is what constitutes the 'push' – work is pushed towards them and somehow they need to find a way to manage (or become a bottleneck, which may very well happen if they are extremely overloaded).

What kind of human being with a brain would not get stressed in such circumstances?

Not having authority to choose work that meets their requirements is one of the fundamental causes for burn out in private practice. Because this means no control over day to day. No agency. Lawyers are just there to handle whatever is thrown at them. How deeply unmotivating.

I have heard many associates calling themselves 'slaves'. Yes, slaves.

How will they ever grow into fulfilled partners if this is how they feel? No wonder that many quit private practice after a few years of feeling like that.

It is time we addressed these issues with intention and understanding, by implementing measures to tackle them.

Why pulling work for yourself is much better

Instead of the 'push', let us imagine the 'pull' type of work flow.

Imagine an associate who is in control of their tasks. Imagine that they are able to choose work from the available pool based on what fits their calendar best and is therefore within their capacity. Remember, they are already motivated to work a lot because of their targets.

Having this authority to choose puts the responsibility on the person to choose work they are able to complete. And if they struggle, it is up to them to find a solution, because, after all, they committed to this (instead of blaming the partner who keeps sending work towards them, even though they are swamped already). After a while, even if the associate in our example did not have the best time management skills to begin with, they will get better at choosing and planning their work. Because no one else will do it for them. They are in control. And they succeed and fail on their own account.

On the other hand, if they have taken up a lot of work because they are excited to work on these cases, even though the amount of effort may be the same or even more as with the 'push' type of system, they would be

Longer term view

much more committed and happy to produce the work as they have made the choice themselves.

Burnout does not happen simply because a person has too much on. It happens because they have no agency over their life. Because they are a victim of their circumstances. They are there just to serve. And therefore they do not feel like they are winning at the game of law.

Push work	**Pull work**
Work is coming at me from all across the firm	Work across the firm is collected in a pool of available matters
I have no authority to say 'no' or negotiate deadlines	I have the authority to choose work that fits my strengths and availability
I am at the mercy of work coming at me and I need to manage somehow (or look weak)	I am in control of my commitments and I need to deliver what I have taken on (to prove myself)
I am a victim of my circumstances	I am winning at the game of law

Lawyers want to be winning at the game of law

Private practice could really benefit from giving more agency to their lawyers and turning the reactive mode more around to proactive.

Instead of pushing, make them pull.

Lawyers feel like they are winning if they have agency to choose work that fits their capabilities, if they can be in sufficient control of their day to day, and if they can strategically develop their expertise.

Of course things will happen and days will become busier than planned. But I do think we could trust lawyers more to have this level of agency. Because this is how we enable them to become self-sufficient, self-motivating and ultimately – partners.

This also creates what I believe to be a healthy competition over work. As an example, if an associate wants to do specific high-value work, it is likely that their colleagues want it as well. This puts them in competition over this kind of work, and they need to figure out how they could get this work in.

Phases of AI adoption at law firms

Perhaps they need to sell themselves to the partner holding the rails of a particular high-value deal? Build up the relationship with them over time? Or build up the relationship with the end client directly? These are all extremely valuable skills for associates later in their career when they want to become partners. So why not let them exercise these!

Instead of pushing them into low agency, why not pull them towards exciting work, give them a feel of competition early on, and therefore enable them to hone in on their 'partner skills'.

> *Let me bring a personal example to illustrate this. When I was an associate, the firm I worked at used to publish new cases each morning at 10 am via a firm-wide automated email update (with confidential cases marked respectively). That was the time of the day when I would be by my computer looking for interesting new cases to work on. If I spotted something promising, I would run to the door of the partner that was managing the case and offer my support. This is how I got to work on some of the biggest cases I have ever been on. And I do not remember complaining about having too much on, because I chose to work on this. So I was committed.*

AI assistant for case management

Let us get back to the AI assistants and the infinite ways they could prove to be instrumental for future lawyers in their day-to-day work.

As another example, let us imagine an AI assistant working on a legal matter alongside a lawyer. An AI assistant trained in project management could help the lawyer keep track of tasks and deadlines. It could also prompt the lawyer on how to best manage the case and the client. While also providing draft communication and documents for doing so.

An average lawyer is not necessarily a great project manager, so such AI assistance could turn out to be quite valuable. The AI assistant can be trained on various project management methods and also on concrete data pulled from previous cases. It can therefore help the lawyer manage the case in the most efficient and attentive way, by learning from past experience and synthesising it to suit the current circumstances.

As a lawyer, it is challenging to constantly stay on top of all the tasks, especially when working across various clients and cases. And while also thinking fast (admin and comms) and thinking slow (analysing). We have all felt how alternating between fast and slow thinking is a real waste of brainpower.

This is where such an AI assistant could prompt the lawyer to check in with the client, or provide a relevant update (after, for example, seeing an incoming email from court on the status of proceedings). It can also provide the draft email.

At the same time, the lawyer can assign admin and comms windows in their day when they are doing many tasks like that at once (fast thinking), and after that getting back to slow thinking.

And, of course, the AI assistant can fill in all the time cards for the lawyer on the go. Because it can keep track of everything the lawyer is working on (that is until we stop billing time altogether).

Such an AI assistant would free up some of the lawyer's time from legal admin, and enable them to instead concentrate on strategic topics and other areas where they are able to bring most value to the client.

By now, we have looked at various AI assistants that could be very beneficial in our day-to-day work as lawyers. However, it needs to be noted that the development of such technologies is a whole other matter. Here we need to follow the tailwinds of technology companies, big and small, and do our best to be at least involved in where their products are going. Because they are going to many places, and they are going fast, with or without us.

Future law firm structure

Inevitably, with the addition of a variety of specifically trained AI tools as 24/7 staff members of a law firm, the structure of law firms is also due to change.

We will no longer have a need for so-called 'pyramid structure' where a small group of partners sit on top, and a large volume of associates and senior associates sit under them. We will simply have much less need for human power to do the heavy paper pushing.

Instead, we can expect to see the emergence of more lean structures – a small group of partners sitting on top and a similarly small group of associates and senior associates sitting under them.

Phases of AI adoption at law firms

The new generation law firm powered by AI will not be a huge behemoth as a current Magic Circle firm, but would more resemble a venture capital firm with a few partners and few associates, all enhanced by latest technologies. This enables the firm to have a smaller overhead, move faster and be more agile to adapting new technology.

This in turn has the potential to further democratise the legal industry, as the entity threshold decreases in terms of human capital, thereby enabling smaller firms to come on the market and compete with the established firms.

Current pyramid structure	**New lean structure**
1 Partner	1 Partner
5 Senior Associates	3 Senior Associates
10 Associates	2 Associates
3 Legal Assistants	Variety of AI tools

Let us see what this means in terms of human capital. In the current pyramid structure, we would need a total of 19 members on the team, whereas in the new lean structure we would only need six lawyers to deliver the same amount of work. That is a reduction of human capital by more than three times. In other words, that is a saving of 13 salaries.

A significant part of this saving will go towards AI tools, especially on the outset of changing from one structure to the other as the upfront cost of onboarding a model is high. However, over time it is easy to see how the new lean structure would pay off in terms of wages saved on the team of lawyers.

The assumption in the new lean structure is that the partner brings in the work and oversees its delivery, while the three senior associates provide the service alongside the partner, thereby doing most of the heavy lifting in terms of work delivery. And the two associates are tech savvy AI tool users who assist senior associates in preparing the bulk of the deliverables.

The above example is of course a simplification and may not directly apply to your practice area. But hopefully it explains how drastically law firm structures are about to change.

We may also start seeing law firms that look more like companies instead of traditional partnerships. As the business model changes in line with the adoption of AI, and as law firms start offering a wider range of technology enhanced services, a new type of value will start accumulating within the business. So alongside human capital, there will also be technology assets that accumulate and depreciate in value, which may in turn attract external investors. This all enables us to reimagine the business model and thereby value creation at the firm.

Chapter 9

Tasks that will remain with human lawyers

As explained in the book, lawyers are well placed to work with AI as we work with the written word every day. We are masterful language processors by profession.

Further to this, lawyers are also suited for so-called prompt engineering. Prompt engineering is a technical term for writing inputs for AI tools that will produce optimal outputs. Essentially this means making sure that the model produces the outcome that we are after. We are well suited to such an approach because this is what we do every day when working with younger colleagues. We give them well considered INSTRUCTIONS and see the RESULTS of our instructions. Good instructions bring good outcomes.

Similarly, AI tools will not give us the answer we are looking for right away in return for a random question. That is an illusion. The value lies in asking the right questions. We need to get to the point of becoming very skilled in asking the questions and also challenging the results.

In order to get the best out of AI we need to work with it the same way we work with younger colleagues. We need to ask good questions and also have the necessary legal expertise to review the outcome. We need to refine the outcome and tweak it where necessary. And iterate until we get to a good result that we are happy with.

The standard work process at most firms between a senior and a junior associate is such where the first gives instructions for the second to produce a particular piece of work. Once the junior associate has put forward their first draft, the senior associate will review it and provide further instructions. This process goes back and forth until the work is approved and sent to the client.

Let us see how AI tools fit into this workflow between a senior and junior associate.

Tasks that will remain with human lawyers

First of all, we can anticipate more tech savvy senior lawyers to work with AI directly, with much less requirement for junior lawyers to do the usual heavy paper lifting. Whereas less tech savvy senior lawyers would be looking to work with junior lawyers who are well versed in using AI, so that they too can get the amplification for their work product. Gradually, we will get to a point where not using AI is like not using the Internet.

Having said that, the work product would still need to be reviewed and vetted by a senior lawyer. It is still the responsibility of licensed lawyers to bring the necessary assurance to legal advice. The machine is not replacing that, at least not in high-stakes situations and when advice is sought from a licenced law firm.

So the workflow in terms of working on a legal matter remains somewhat similar (at least until the law firm business model is wholly changed). Let us now look at other qualities that are innate to human lawyers and therefore harder to replace by a machine.

9.1 RELATIONSHIP BUILDING AND MANAGEMENT

While AI will incredibly amplify our output as lawyers, there are some very human qualities that will still remain in the hands of lawyers. By that I mean building trust and relationships with our clients.

The reality of today is that there are a lot of smart lawyers. And the quality of legal service is quite good on average. Yes, there is great quality on the one end of the scale and poor quality on the other end, but in the middle we have thousands of lawyers and hundreds of law firms that consistently deliver good quality work.

It does not really matter for a client whether they engage firm A or firm B on a day-to-day legal matter. I dare to say such a decision often comes down to relationships – who does the client have a good working relationship with? That would often be their first natural point of contact for new instruction.

Relationships take time to build and start with establishing trust. After we have established trust we need to put in the time and attention to build the relationship. And as long as we have human clients, we will need to build relationships between humans.

Having said that, I do like to think about a future where client AI talks to lawyer AI and there is no person-to person-relationship. But that is for another time.

9.2 UNDERSTANDING OF NUANCES, CONTEXT AND ETHICS

Lawyers understand the nuances, context, and implications of legal concepts. Their reasoning includes moral, ethical, and practical considerations, which require deep understanding and critical thinking. Whereas, AI tools do not understand context in a human sense. They provide output based on their input and programming, rather than actual comprehension of the matter at hand. They lack genuine understanding and the ability to reason beyond their training data.

Similarly, lawyers exercise critical judgement, weighing various factors and making decisions based on a combination of legal knowledge, experience, and professional intuition. Rather, AI tools lack the ability to exercise judgement. Their responses are generated based on patterns and probabilities.

Finally, lawyers are bound by ethical codes and professional responsibilities. They must consider the broader impact of their advice and actions on clients, society, and the legal system. Whereas AI tools do not have innate ethical considerations. Their outputs are purely the result of algorithms and data without regard for the consequences.

In summary, lawyers bring understanding, critical thinking, ethical judgement, and adaptability to their work, whereas AI tools operate based on patterns in data without genuine comprehension or responsibility.

9.3 HUMAN EXPERTISE AND CREATIVITY

A true hallmark of a senior lawyer is the ability to take a 30-page complex legal document and scan through it within 30 seconds to check any red flags and other important points. That is where experience gets you.

Even with the increasing use of AI, we should not leave this capability aside as nothing beats experience. Not even an extremely capable AI tool.

Added to this, we need to keep in mind that AI tools do not have real life experience. Kind of the same way as we did not have it when we graduated from law school. But even more so. One might even argue that AI tools do not have common sense. Now that is an issue, and something we should always keep in mind when we work with technology.

There is another very human quality that AI tools miss – that is, creativity. Every lawyer knows that sometimes the answer is not obvious at all.

Tasks that will remain with human lawyers

Sometimes particular circumstances call for a bit of legal creativity (within the boundaries of the law, of course).

The best lawyers know that no legal situation is impossible. Quite to the contrary – it is often possible to get to yes (or at least maybe), if we try hard enough.

In order to solve seemingly impossible situations, we need to pull from our internal resources of creativity. This may entail clever problem solving, or moving across domains and pulling knowledge from related fields, where it makes sense. Taking the variables of a particular legal situation and moving them around in all imaginable ways to get to a different outcome.

No AI tool is able to do any of that. That alone is why lawyers should not worry that AI will take all of our bread away. As long as the legal world revolves around humans – as long as humans adopt laws and pass judgement – human oversight is needed to deal with the complexities of the law.

9.4 PROBLEM SOLVING, STRATEGISING AND NEGOTIATIONS

While AI tools are great for sparring ideas and brainstorming, they can only go so far as they are detached from the 'real world'. AI tools also do not have the very human qualities that enable us to get to 'the bigger picture view'. Such a view means understanding the many factors of a given situation, and also the interdependencies among such factors. It can be quite a creative exercise where we need to draw from our understanding of the relevant legal domain, but also may need to move across domains.

It is a trait of a senior lawyer to be able to enter a situation, gather information, and come up with a plan on how to solve it. It usually involves mapping down all of the variables, positions of each relevant side, and the desired outcome. Negotiation is a big part of it as it is often the means to getting to the desired outcome.

It is still the human being who can bring their experience and gut feeling into a difficult situation. Into a situation with no evident available solution. This is where seasoned professionals thrive thanks to the years of experience they have under their belt. They have seen versions of similar situations before. And they are able to draw from it in order to come up with a strategy on how to deal with it.

Problem solving, strategising and negotiations

All of the above is useful in contract negotiations prior to signing, but also post signing if a dispute arises between the parties. As long as we still have to enter into agreements, or exit from them, between human beings, we will need to deal with it on a human level. It is also helpful in overall strategising for the business. And in litigation strategy as well.

Essentially, the tasks that require creative and expansive thinking will remain with human lawyers and will remain high in value.

It is the human mind that is able to grasp situations and come up with solutions without having to know all of the variables and without having absolute clarity on all of the details. A seasoned professional is able to think in terms of first principles – what is really going on here, what does the other side want, and what does my client want. And how to get as close to what my client wants as possible.

Such problem-solving situations can be extremely interesting and engaging. As they often require true human creativity. Let me bring an example.

> Let us imagine that our client is an investor that has invested money in a company and in return has received rights to some shares in the said company. Now let us say that the other shareholders of this company want to squeeze our client out, for whatever reason. Perhaps they do not want to share the proceeds of the business with the client. So, in order to do that they establish a new company and move all the business there, leaving behind no value for our client in the original company.
>
> The client comes to us, and is of course upset. So what do we do? We first look into the existing documentation. Perhaps there is an investment agreement, or a shareholders agreement. But perhaps there is nothing. Say we do not find anything that would explicitly address the current situation and help our client. And the other shareholders are simply saying our client has no rights over their new company.
>
> This is where problem solving starts. We have a situation that is somewhat difficult and that has no immediate clear answer. The contract does not say anything. The other side denies everything. This is a perfect situation for human capabilities in a lawyer. If you are a corporate lawyer reading that, you are probably already thinking in terms of potential strategy for the client. Hint: we need to seek help from legal principles.

> *In all honesty, I do not think experienced lawyers have much to fear when it comes to AI. They only have much to win in terms of enhancing their day-to-day service delivery. Once a lawyer has become an expert in a specific area, and provided that this specific area still continues to be relevant for the world at large, the lawyer will have work to do and will have clients to look after.*

9.5 MARKETING AND SALES

We can expect legal marketing and sales to move away from a template approach (legal directories and such) towards a more client-centric approach. We can also expect client-to-lawyer interactions to become much more important.

While the law firm brand still continues to matter, it will not be enough to sustain a strong practice over the long term. On the other hand, the firm's brand can be greatly amplified by some of its key lawyers and their personal brands and relationships.

While relationships move online, they tend to also become more personal. It is somewhat counterintuitive, but it seems to be easier for us to open up online as opposed to face to face, while also reaching a much wider audience. A strong public brand often means sharing parts of your thinking publicly, almost exposing yourself to an extent. That provides an opportunity for your audience to relate to you (and approve of you or judge you).

We should not discount the importance of personal brand over firm brand in the near future. There are many, many, many reputable law firms out there. So how do you stand out? By having lawyers with strong personal brands. They will then also amplify your firm's brand.

We can expect clients to judge the firm's values based on the values of its lawyers. Because after all, the firm itself does not have values, the people who make up the firm do. Which is why clever firms with a few or even just one lawyer with strong values and solid public reach will inevitably stand out to prospective clients.

The new generation clients do not want to hear from the senior partner. They do not want to look up to their service providers. Instead, they want

Marketing and sales

to do business with their peers thereby supporting their own network. We can also expect there to be a fair amount of resistance or even resentment towards the status quo, because after all, this is simply part of the generational overtake. The firms that will survive are the ones who give the new generation a stake and a say in the business. Even better yet, who publicly identify with their up and coming faces.

Please refer to **Appendix 2** for AI tools useful in marketing endeavours.

Afterword

Advice to young lawyers

We tend to put so much emphasis on legal education and on becoming the smartest lawyer in the room. In reality, being a smart lawyer is not enough to have real success in law. Sometimes, being very smart can even have the opposite effect – we might get stuck 'in the weeds' too much, endlessly obsessing over every detail instead of looking at the bigger picture.

Becoming a fully rounded professional, not just a lawyer, is crucial for our careers. Alongside legal expertise, it is similarly important to develop other qualities, like our understanding of business and human nature. The more we have exposure to different legal matters, senior lawyers and clients, the more we can educate our world view. A young lawyer should be like a sponge – noticing everything and trying to make sense of it while remaining flexible in their thinking and open to alternative views.

But first of all, inevitably, we need to become good lawyers. That takes practice and a lot of patience. Admittedly, that may also mean completing boring tasks for several years. So it helps to have realistic expectations.

LEARN FROM THE BEST

While it is important to go to the best law school you can possibly access, school does not really prepare us for work as a lawyer. Law firms do. Which is why it is crucial to work at the best firm you can possibly get into as a young lawyer for at least two to three years. This is where you will feel in your own skin what it means to deliver quality legal work. And that feeling will always stay with you, you will build an inner compass for what quality work feels like.

It is equally important to work with senior lawyers that are excellent in their work. Often, we can find the most brilliant lawyers at top law firms, which is why it is necessary to get into there. Once in, try to get as much exposure as you can to different partners and their style of delivering legal services. Find the one that you think is the best – someone who shares your values and whom you can look up to for years to come. If you cannot find

Advice to young lawyers

someone like that, change firms. Do not settle for a mediocre role model, because this sets the North Star for the rest of your career. This cannot be emphasised enough – who you look up to is who you will become. So choose wisely and aim high. Once you find your ideal role model, do everything you can to get exposure to them – be helpful in their day to day and build trust with them.

START BY BEING HELPFUL, IN ORDER TO BECOME VALUABLE

As a young lawyer, your main client is an older colleague who gives you work. While it is easy to think that, after years in law school, we know a thing or two about law, the reality is we do not. All of us need to go through an apprenticeship period, there is no avoiding that. So the best approach you can take for your own benefit is to be helpful towards more senior colleagues and build a reputation for being reliable. Being reliable means doing what you said you would do. It also means doing proper work when a task is assigned to you.

During your first years, you are entirely dependable on senior colleagues. It is best to acknowledge that as part of the journey, earn their trust and build relationships with them. This also means you need to be flexible and perhaps lower your expectations. Work at law firms moves at a very fast pace, and senior colleagues do not often have time to explain every step to you, and give perfect instructions. Therefore, if something remains unclear – ask. But also learn to anticipate their requests and build sensitivity towards how they are doing. This will become very useful once you start working with clients directly. Servicing senior colleagues well builds up your capability to service clients well later on.

It may sound unfair but young lawyers are easily replaceable. There are a lot of smart lawyers out there. You can, however, start to become valuable if you are easy to work with, reliable and generally produce good work. It takes years to build a reputation at a firm. Your senior colleagues have worked with tens of young lawyers just like you. So how do you stand out? Why should they give work to you?

It is also worth keeping in mind that senior colleagues have a lot of say in your early destiny. They will be asked for feedback on you by the partners. They can advance your career (or not). They can put you forward for an important assignment, or even promotion. Again, it helps to remember – if you have less than five years of experience in law, you do not really call the shots. Your senior colleagues do.

Being a young lawyer means constantly learning and often being the one with the least knowledge. Your senior colleagues have seen much more than you. They know much better how the firm works. They can also understand clients well. So it is best to assume that you do not know much and adapt a learning mindset.

It is also very helpful to your career prospects to find an older colleague who would mentor you. Again, you cannot go at it with the attitude of requesting. They are busy, why should they care? Go at it with the attitude of asking questions and helping them. And try to absorb as much wisdom as you can. It is also helpful to spend time with your colleagues outside work and go to client events that the firm is organising. You should not underestimate socialising even if you mostly work remotely. Networking skills will serve you very well in your career.

FIND YOUR FIELD

Try out different practice areas until you find the one that is best suited for your innate strengths. Law is a long game, so you want to specialise in something that you can become great at and enjoy for years to come. But while you are at it, do not make the mistake of becoming too specialised in a narrow niche. Unless you have scientific aspirations, that would diminish your future outlook to make good moves.

Let me touch upon my journey, in the hopes that it will show the importance of trying out different fields. As a newly qualified attorney I was convinced that I wanted to become a litigation lawyer. Because I like to make my case, the thrill of the race and admittedly I also like to win. However, after having been on a couple of court cases, having smelled the dusty air in courtrooms, I realised I actually do not like it. Most of all I did not like the zero-sum nature of litigation – if I win, then this means someone loses.

So litigation did not feel great. I then switched into corporate law pretty much through happenstance as there was an opening at the firm. Even though I found corporate law lacking a certain level of excitement for me, I did stick with it for quite a few years. Being a young lawyer often means doing boring stuff, for years. Only by doing the work and sticking with the profession can we develop proper expertise. But while we are at it, it is worth keeping one eye open for exciting opportunities.

It so happened that the corporate team was merged with the M&A team at the firm I was with. I had no control over it, it just happened while I was there. And this made my career. I could tell there was something for me in there, even though I had never been on a transaction before. So I started to build up experience and eventually expertise in transactions. By that time, I had been with the firm already for several years. I had earned a level of trust and seniority. So I went all in and paved my way into M&A. I showed a lot of initiative and learned extremely fast. And I found a great role model that I still respect to this day.

Transactions are the most perfect place for me. They have kept me challenged and fulfilled for many years. I love the thrill of a deal. I love to take control of projects and manage them towards a positive outcome. To win when everyone else is winning too.

I could not have planned for it. I mostly achieved it by sticking with the path and taking opportunities when I noticed them. And my corporate experience still helps me as a hedge against bad markets – when transactions are down, corporate restructuring is usually up. So I will always have work. And having initially been in litigation enables me to quickly think in terms of 'what is the worst possible outcome here' as the ultimate test in any complex situation.

A career in law can be long and fulfilling, if approached with an open mind and curiosity.

ADOPT A CLIENT SERVICE MINDSET

If you are a young lawyer and you have worked at a top law firm for a few years, shift your focus from quality legal advice to quality client service – it will pay off. By that time, you are probably already delivering good enough legal advice, improving upon that to perfection will not give the same return in terms of career opportunities, than building your client skills. Learn how to win clients over, learn how to communicate very well, lean into networking, and really just put yourself out there with your face towards clients (both, current and potential).

Law firms concentrate so much on raising young lawyers who deliver quality legal advice. But very little attention, if at all, is given to raising the next generation partners. However, client skills are the ones that are much more likely to make you a partner down the line, than mere legal expertise. Remember that running a law firm is business. The partners running a law firm are business people. If you want to one day be a partner yourself, you need to learn the ropes of business.

Law firm business skills broadly consist of winning new clients over, retaining existing clients, leading a team of lawyers, and the day-to-day operational skills (accounts, budgets, etc). Start by finding opportunities to get more direct exposure to clients – calling them, having meetings with them, always trying to say something relevant and useful. Do not just sit around and wait for the partner to do all the talking and give you a writing assignment. Adopt a mindset to always ask at least one question or make at least one relevant comment at every meeting you are present. As you show more initiative, good partners will notice that and you will naturally get more exposure to clients and more authority in your work with them.

Also remember to work across teams and practice areas as much as you can. This will get you exposure to different clients in different industries, thereby further broadening your understanding of the legal services market.

ADOPT A DAILY PRACTICE TO REFLECT

Once we set our minds on something, it becomes much more clear to us what we need to do in order to achieve our goals. If you want to become an outstanding lawyer, it is advisable to adopt a daily practice where at the end of each day you reflect on what went well and what could be improved, and write it down. Being aware of what needs further work is a significant step towards actually doing the work.

Self reflection, combined with input from more senior lawyers, is a good path towards becoming better every day and therefore advancing closer to your goals. As you progress in terms of seniority, you can add various metrics to such daily reflection (like billables, revenue, and other requirements to advance in career). It is a habit worth cultivating early on.

TRY OUT DIFFERENT CAREER PATHS

There are many different routes available, and until you know for sure, try out several of them. After you have laid a strong foundation, it is fine to change firms, it is fine to go inhouse, it is fine to go solo, it is even fine to become an entrepreneur. All of these different roles show you a different facet of 'law in action' and are useful for developing a fully rounded approach. There is something to learn from every experience, as long as we do not get too comfortable and lower our standards too much. In this day and age we can have several careers during our lifetimes. Inside and

Advice to young lawyers

outside of law. A career in law could also be a good foundation for moving into business.

You should want to learn and evolve into someone who can tackle any legal question across domains. Someone who understands risks intuitively because you have seen so many. And who also understands business enough to be able to think in both, legal and business terms. Law as a standalone thing does not drive anything. Business drives decisions. Business drives change. Law can enable that, support that, or also be in the way. It is therefore important to build an understanding of law around business.

AVOID THE 'SPECIALIST TRAP' AND THE 'LAW FIRM TRAP'

Often the smartest, most hardworking lawyers are prone to fall for the 'specialist trap'. We become experts in our corner of the law and get very, very good at it. It is a trap because along the way we may neglect to learn other skills which are crucial in business – like communication, networking, sales, etc. And if we did not learn these other skills, we may feel like we have no other path available to us but to stay a great expert in our corner of the law. This is a fallacy. The 'specialist trap' is why some of the best lawyers are deeply unhappy – because they do the same thing all over again hundreds of times and at some point, it loses its flavour. And they think they have no other option available to them.

Let me take the 'specialist trap' even deeper within the legal practice. The issue with law firms is that they train us to become 'extreme specialists' in niche areas of expertise. This narrows our future outlooks proportionally – the more specialists we become in something, say in competition law, the less career options we have outside of that. You may find yourself doing one merger clearance after another, and quite enjoying it, while also realising that you really do not have other legal skills. Sometimes the deepest specialists can be embarrassingly shallow generalists, because they have not been exposed to much else than their narrow area of specialisation.

There is also the 'law firm trap' to watch out for. As we stay with the firm and progress in our careers, we are essentially rewarded when abiding to a set of rules, which often tend to be very stringent. As an example, we may become very afraid to make mistakes because we remember vividly the few occasions when we made a mistake and were scrutinised for it by the partner. This takes away from creativity and enthusiasm towards work, as we have the fear of making mistakes constantly at the back of our mind.

This also significantly reduces our future outlook in business as we have become too risk averse.

We may also become reluctant to speak up unless we are absolutely certain that we have the correct answer. Because we do not want to look foolish, and yet again, we are afraid of making mistakes. Speaking up and brainstorming is an important part of getting to the right answer. If we do not do that, we limit our opportunities in terms of working through a variety of potential solutions (some of which may be unrealistic).

Now, this may lead to one of the worst things – being afraid to ask questions. Asking a lot of questions is a crucial part of getting to the bottom of a complex situation. Some of the questions may be irrelevant, but we may want to ask them anyway to make sure we have uncovered all of the aspects of the matter. Now, if we are afraid to ask questions, then we may omit to uncover something, and ultimately provide a half-way or even entirely unsuitable solution to the client.

GOING FOR A PARTNER, OR NOT

Several years in, if you then feel very strongly that you want to invest up to ten years to build out a law firm career, then make a realistic plan to go after it and stick to it. Find out about the requirements and start working towards achieving them. Keep an open discussion with the firm and be clear on your trajectory.

This means that you need to clearly ask your partner what it takes to become a partner yourself. What are the qualities you need to develop? What are the specific requirements? There is no point in sitting around and thinking someone will notice you and give you a lift up. That is simply not going to happen. So once you have set your sights, show ambition. Also show willingness to work hard to achieve the goals. And ask for help as much as you can, you are going to need it.

But do not just do it because you think this is what you are supposed to do. There are a lot of lawyers working at top firms for a lot of money while being absolutely miserable. While it is easy to say that this is the fault of the firms, it is also the fault of the lawyers for not making better decisions for themselves.

So it really is about figuring out what works for you. And daring to make a change if something no longer works.

LEGAL CAREER OUTSIDE LAW FIRMS

This may sound controversial but some of the best lawyers, who have had a lot of success in their professional lives, tend not to be the smartest lawyers on the outset. They tend to have cultivated other high-quality characteristics. Like being a great public speaker. Being a great networker. Being great at something that most lawyers are not great at – that is their competitive edge.

As lawyers we spend so much effort trying to become the smartest in the room, but on the leadership level we will mostly meet other lawyers that are not necessarily the smartest in strictly specialist terms. Instead, they have honed in on other skills alongside 'being a lawyer'.

The managing partner of a law firm is not the smartest lawyer in every legal domain. They have other skills like emotional intelligence and winning people over. Not to speak of business skills that are crucial.

Similarly, a general counsel is someone that has honed in on their understanding of risks across domains and across borders, and their capability to explain it to the rest of the business consisting of non-lawyers. Also, they have an ability to make risk-aware decisions.

Around 70 per cent of general counsel work is business, with 30 per cent being law.

That is worth thinking about – what could you be so great at that most other lawyers would not even stand a chance? Or are simply not cultivating these skills because they are too busy being smart.

I do believe all characteristics can be developed over time, but it is best to start with those that are already innate to you. Best to amplify on your existing strengths and cultivate your competitive advantage that is specific to you.

INCREASING AREAS OF EXPERTISE

Instead of participating in the race for popular jobs with all the other highly qualified lawyers, it is worthwhile for young lawyers to lean into new areas of expertise that are emerging around us. Such new fields inevitably have less competition and therefore it is possible to progress to the top faster there. There is not much point in doing something that everyone else is doing, unless you want to be in competition with everyone else over jobs that are inevitably in smaller numbers than the lawyers that apply for them.

New technologies bring along new demand for legal expertise. Here are some of the areas that are rapidly increasing in terms of demand and still relatively low in expertise and therefore competition among lawyers: everything relating to blockchain, digital assets, tokenisation of traditional assets, digital identity, AI – just to name some of the main areas.

Blockchain innovation is already having an overarching impact in traditional finance and other related fields, and it will only expand from this point onwards. It is worth getting into these new areas of legal expertise because not so many lawyers have capitalised on them yet. And if you position yourself well as a specialist, you may find forward thinking employers competing for your talent.

Therefore, on top of doing what you like and are good at, it is also worth thinking in terms of where you would have the highest upside and lowest competition to your specific skills and experience. This ensures that you can gradually move towards the top jobs in your chosen field, and may have a faster track towards becoming a partner or a general counsel.

USE AI AS YOUR SECOND BRAIN

AI is your biggest competitive advantage and career accelerator. Use it every day. Use it for everything you can think of. Use it as your second brain. Please refer to **Appendix 2** for specific AI tools and master all of them for the best competitive advantage on the legal market.

By mastering AI, you will future proof your career. Your senior colleagues will value you. Also, you will never have to deal with the 'blank page fear'.

It is not often that young lawyers can get an advantage that bypasses the regular 'ten years to become a fully rounded lawyer' route. It is the first time something so tangible has come along. I wish I had artificial intelligence when I started off, I could have saved several years along the way.

When the Internet first came along, the young lawyers with 'Internet skills' were quite valuable in the market. There was also a time when email skills, word processing skills and Outlook skills were seen as a valuable quality in a new hire. The same is happening with AI tools and all the skills that come with it (eg, prompt engineering). Young lawyers with great AI skills are becoming increasingly valuable. In due course, this will become a core 'lawyer skill'.

So it is well worth honing in on your use of AI tools, using them every day, and really mastering these tools. And putting it on your CV as one of your core skills.

When I gave a lecture to law students at Cambridge University, I was asked how one is supposed to become a senior lawyer in the AI era, when senior lawyers have less need for junior lawyers as apprentices since they now have AI tools instead.

I still think that becoming a fully rounded senior lawyer takes more than five years of practising law. However, instead of primarily learning from older colleagues, I expect younger lawyers to now learn mostly from their work with AI. AI tools have a lot of knowledge and can be great teachers and mentors for younger lawyers. So, alongside learning from a senior colleague, learn from AI. Such AI mentors can be different and plentiful, providing a fully rounded legal training. They can widen university education and mock practical work experience.

NAVIGATING IN UNCERTAIN TERRAIN

As a final piece of advice, I would like to touch upon the three pillars of competitive legal approach that I have come up with for young lawyers and that really are applicable to all lawyers no matter the stage of our careers. The pillars are:

I – Understanding of fundamental legal principles across domains

II – High-level risk and reward-based thinking

III – Learning fast from available pool of knowledge

I find this approach useful in navigating uncharted territories as a legal professional. This is especially relevant in finding our way in emerging fields like Web 3 and all it encompasses.

Let us look at these pillars more closely.

Pillar I

Pillar I – the absolute 'must have' foundation that is worth cultivating is a strong understanding of legal principles across domains.

These principles are (a) universal and (b) domain specific. We do not want to break these in any event, because this is where we go wrong and get into difficult terrain.

This approach is extremely helpful in areas where there is not much specific regulation. The legal principles still apply and we can draw from them to guide us through. They also help us to anticipate future regulation (because it will be built upon these same foundational principles).

As an example, there is a principle in finance relating to consumer protection. It basically assumes that the average consumer has a low understanding of financial products and therefore should be protected against unwisely losing their money. The same principle can be applied to 'new finance' brought about by blockchain, even though it may not be clearly written in the relevant regulation yet.

Pillar II

Pillar II – high-level risk and reward-based thinking.

This is where we take the principles and move horizontally in search of risks and solutions. It is all about asking the important questions to uncover the relevant risks.

In the same example, knowing the consumer protection principle from finance, we can look at the new blockchain project and ask the relevant questions to uncover potential risks (eg, is the project geared towards consumers?).

Pillar III

Pillar III – learning fast from the available pool of knowledge.

We as lawyers tend to be set in our ways. That approach is no longer serving us. We need the agility to quickly learn and constantly improve our

Advice to young lawyers

approach. The world around us is changing at an ever-increasing pace, and we need to keep up with it. Technology can greatly aid us here.

In summary, always be grounded in logic and first principles. Never deviate or dismiss these. Practice problem solving in everything you do. This is the foundation of legal work.

Appendices

Appendix 1

AI-generated executive summaries

Here is an executive summary of each part of the book as generated by proprietary AI. Feel free to use it to compare against your main takeaways of the book. You can think whether you agree with the AI or not, and let me know!

EXECUTIVE SUMMARY OF PART 1: WHAT DO CLIENTS NEED?

Chapter 1: Clients need to be able to trust their lawyer

Trust as a Fundamental Need: Trust is essential in the lawyer-client relationship, forming a human bond that validates and supports the adherence to professional advice. Lawyers often overlook interpersonal skills critical for fostering long-term, sustainable relationships. Trust enhances client retention, satisfaction, and professional growth.

Clients in Stressful Situations: Clients often approach lawyers during high-stress situations requiring comfort and rapid response. The busyness and over-scheduling of lawyers can delay response times, leading to dissatisfaction and exacerbating clients' stressful circumstances. Prompt acknowledgment of client concerns is essential, even if immediate resolution isn't possible.

Communication: Effective communication is vital in building trust. A prompt response to enquiries, even if only to acknowledge receipt, reassures clients of their importance. Consistent updates and clarity, especially in stressful legal matters, are crucial in maintaining confidence and trust.

Responsiveness: Quick responsiveness to client requests is critical. Immediate recognition and reassurance are paramount for clients facing urgent legal issues. Timely responses, even to set expectations for further communication, can mitigate client anxiety and dissatisfaction.

Face-to-Face Interactions: Despite digital advancements, personal interactions remain irreplaceable. Regular in-person meetings strengthen

AI-generated executive summaries

trust and ensure clients feel genuinely supported, reinforcing their reliance on their lawyer's counsel.

The Role of AI in Building Trust: AI tools indirectly enhance client relationships by managing routine tasks, freeing lawyers to engage more directly with clients. This allows for increased availability and focus on personal interactions, crucial for trust-building.

Efficiency in Legal Work: AI significantly boosts legal work efficiency by streamlining tasks like research, analysis, and drafting. This efficiency enables lawyers to devote more time to client communication and relationship building, improving service quality and outcomes.

Prioritising Human Interaction: Despite AI's benefits, the human element remains crucial. Clients are more likely to remember and value the personal support they receive over specific legal advice. AI should support, not replace, the personal aspects of legal services, ensuring clients feel appreciated and well-supported.

Mutual Benefits of Trust-Based Relationships: Building trust fosters mutually beneficial relationships. Clients who feel well-supported are more likely to return and refer others, enhancing the lawyer's professional success and job satisfaction. Direct, personal interactions not only support clients but also enrich the lawyer's professional experience.

Reputation and Client Referrals: A lawyer's reputation for trust and effective communication often precedes them, opening doors to new client referrals. Trust-based relationships are key to sustaining long-term success in the legal field.

In conclusion, while AI can augment efficiency, the cornerstone of successful legal practice is the ability to build and maintain trust through proactive communication, responsiveness, and personal engagement. These practices ensure clients feel valued and supported, leading to enduring, reciprocal relationships.

Chapter 2: Clients need to be able to rely on their lawyer

Core Client Need for Support

Comprehensive Support: Clients expect their lawyers to act as partners who offer active support, not merely service providers. Effective support

Executive summary of Part 1: What do clients need?

involves excellent communication – being prompt, clear, and consistently updating on progress. Support also requires a personal touch, such as direct communication of bad news and transparency about fees. Lawyers often get too caught up in daily tasks to provide the necessary support, leading to client frustration.

Client Workload and Stress: Clients, especially in-house counsels like GCs, manage numerous legal and non-legal matters simultaneously. They depend on external counsels to take ownership of legal issues, easing their workload. Insufficient updates or clarity from lawyers can increase stress and damage the trust in the partnership.

Practical Legal Support: Legal support must address practical business needs and be understandable. Documents overloaded with complex disclaimers and assumptions leave clients confused and uncertain. Lawyers need to provide clear, practical advice to truly alleviate client concerns.

Enhancing Client Support

Clarity and Simplicity in Communication: Effective lawyers distil complex legal topics into concise, understandable notes. Legal advice should be straightforward and accessible, particularly for clients without legal backgrounds. Lawyers should focus on delivering solutions in ways that are helpful and relieving to the client.

Status Updates and Proactive Management: Clients should not have to manage their lawyers. Regular, brief status updates can reassure clients and demonstrate proficient handling of legal matters. Clear and concise communication is essential.

Tailoring Legal Advice: Legal advice should be customised to reflect the client's specific context and needs, enhancing the client-lawyer relationship.

The Role of AI in Supporting Clients

Refining Communication: AI can enhance the clarity of legal communications by eliminating unnecessary jargon and refining complex drafts. This helps ensure that clients understand their legal standing and the advice provided.

Future Communication Improvements: AI could revolutionise client-lawyer interactions by ensuring clear and precise communication,

AI-generated executive summaries

potentially through AI agents that represent lawyers and clients, improving understanding and implementation of legal advice.

In conclusion, clients need reliable legal partners who manage and simplify their legal challenges effectively. Communication, tailored advice, and strategic use of AI are key to providing the support that clients need and value.

Chapter 3: Clients need to save legal costs

Core Client Need to Save Costs

Value Justification: Clients often struggle to see the direct value of legal functions, which typically prevent risks rather than generate direct revenue. Legal costs are scrutinised against strict budgets, requiring justifications that align with visible business benefits.

Current Billing Model: Lawyers usually aim to bill 6–8 hours daily, involving tasks like research and document drafting – referred to as 'heavy paper lifting.' The transition towards fixed-fee structures challenges lawyers to maintain profitability while meeting traditional billing targets.

Strategies to Be Cost-Savvy

Working Within Budgets: Lawyers should align their services with clients' budgets, providing cost-effective solutions. Transparency in billing and acknowledging when another provider may offer better value can build trust and long-term client relationships.

Value-Oriented Billing: Billing should reflect the client's perceived value, considering the business impact rather than just time spent. Strategic decisions, like choosing to settle a case early, can save clients money and enhance a lawyer's reputation for future engagements.

Transparency and Communication: Clear communication about fees and potential overruns is essential. Personalised billing notes can foster better client relations and improve compliance with payment terms.

How AI Can Enhance Cost Efficiency

Reducing Manual Labour: AI can reduce the time lawyers spend on routine tasks, allowing more focus on strategic activities. This efficiency helps firms adapt to fixed fee structures by lowering the cost of legal services.

Executive summary of Part 2: New generation lawyers

Rethinking Billing Models: The integration of AI in legal work suggests a shift from hourly billing to potentially fixed fees for AI-driven tasks. Firms will need innovative pricing strategies that reflect AI's role in service delivery.

Client Expectations and AI: Clients increasingly expect that efficiencies from AI will be reflected in their legal bills. Law firms might need to develop proprietary AI solutions and consider how to charge for AI's contributions to legal work.

Future of AI in Legal Billing: AI's increasing role could standardise new billing practices, including fixed fees for AI tasks or retainers for ongoing AI usage. This evolution requires law firms to reassess their value propositions and billing methods to ensure they align with modern technological capabilities and client expectations.

In conclusion, as demand for cost efficiency grows, law firms must leverage AI to streamline operations and rethink billing models. This approach will not only meet client expectations for value but also promote sustainable, trust-based relationships.

EXECUTIVE SUMMARY OF PART 2: NEW GENERATION LAWYERS

Chapter 4: Lawyers as language engineers

The chapter advocates for a transformation in legal writing, emphasising the importance of clarity and directness to meet the practical needs of clients. It suggests that embracing AI tools can significantly enhance the ability to draft precise and understandable legal documents, moving away from the traditional, often convoluted legal language that can obscure meaning and intent. This shift is crucial as the legal profession evolves, ensuring lawyers remain effective communicators in an increasingly complex world.

Dealing with the Written Word: Lawyers are referred to as 'language engineers' due to their daily engagement with the written word, from legislation to contracts. They are tasked with interpreting these texts, synthesising them with client-specific knowledge, and providing clear, written responses. The precision of language in law is crucial, as even synonyms can carry vastly different legal implications.

AI-generated executive summaries

The Style of Legal Writing: Historically, legal writing has been influenced by traditions from Roman oratory and philosophy, often characterised by elaborate and sometimes archaic language. This style, while rhetorically impressive, can be problematic from a client's perspective. Overly complex language, while potentially serving as a literary masterpiece, can hinder practical understanding and application, making it commercially unfeasible.

Client-Centric Writing: The challenge lies in the legal profession's tendency to produce documents that are verbose and packed with jargon, which may not only lead to misunderstandings but also disputes over contractual intentions. A more straightforward and clear writing style helps prevent these issues, making legal documents more accessible and easier to negotiate for those outside the legal profession.

The Shift to Clear Legal Drafting: Effective legal writing should serve the needs of businesses and laypersons, not just lawyers. This means producing documents that are clear and concise, allowing clients to grasp their content quickly without multiple readings. Lawyers should aim to simplify complexity rather than add to it, ensuring their writings are practical and actionable.

Using AI Tools to Improve Clarity: AI tools represent a significant advancement in legal writing, helping to overcome challenges referred to as the 'blank page block' or the 'template fallacy.' These tools can generate documents based on sophisticated templates or precedents, reducing dependency on outdated methods and improving drafting efficiency. AI assists in ensuring documents are not only technically accurate but also clear and concise, reflecting the needs of modern legal practice.

Chapter 5: Lawyers as data processors

AI tools represent a transformative shift in how lawyers process data and manage legal tasks. By integrating AI, lawyers can focus on higher level strategic work and client interactions, ensuring that their roles evolve with technological advancements. The chapter emphasises the need for quality control in AI tools and suggests that lawyers must adapt to these changes to remain efficient and relevant in their practices.

Conducting Legal Analysis and Drafting Documents: Lawyers function as human data processors, spending considerable time on legal research and document management. This includes reviewing case files, contracts, and

Executive summary of Part 2: New generation lawyers

managing discovery in litigation. Legal research supports case arguments and precedents, encompassing both billable and non-billable hours.

Brain Functionality in Lawyers: Research shows lawyers exhibit heightened activity in brain areas related to analytical thinking and logical reasoning, essential for decision-making and handling complex information. This ability is comparable to London taxi drivers' navigational skills, although lawyers focus on retaining extensive legal knowledge.

Enhancing Speed with AI Tools: Lawyers' cognitive processes are akin to AI operations, which store and retrieve data methodically. AI tools are trained on vast legal texts, enabling them to generate responses and documents quickly, mirroring a lawyer's thought process but with enhanced reliability and less bias.

Practical Applications of AI in Legal Work: AI significantly boosts productivity in legal settings:

- Transcribing Meetings: AI tools can transcribe meetings verbatim, allowing lawyers to focus more on interaction cues rather than note-taking. These tools can summarise discussions and outline action points.

- Legal Research: AI tools revolutionise legal research by providing refined search results and summarising information, which previously took hours.

- Drafting and Project Management: AI improves drafting efficiency through templates and can manage complex projects like contract negotiations, reducing manual workload and potential errors.

AI in Legal Education and Training: AI's integration into legal education can prepare new lawyers by simulating complex legal scenarios and providing interactive, real-time learning experiences. This approach enhances understanding and application of legal principles in practical settings.

Chapter 6: Lawyers as therapists

Lawyers, while trained to be analytical and detached, must also cultivate empathy while also considering their own mental health. Balancing professionalism with empathy can lead to more effective client relationships and personal satisfaction in legal practice. The chapter advocates for a more human-centric approach to law, where understanding and addressing both the legal and emotional needs of clients can coexist with maintaining personal well-being and professional integrity.

The Role of Empathy in Legal Practice: In private practice, lawyers often act as both counsellors and advisors to clients who approach them with crucial personal or business matters. The effectiveness of legal service delivery extends beyond the content of advice to how it is communicated, necessitating a balance of professional detachment and empathy. However, the perception that lawyers lack empathy is prevalent, attributed to the necessity for them to remain composed under stress, potentially making them appear unemotional or distant.

Delivering Difficult Messages: The skill in delivering difficult messages lies not only in the content but significantly in the approach. Lawyers spend much time mastering the content of their legal advice but may overlook the importance of empathetic delivery. Understanding the personal impact of legal outcomes on clients, like the implications of a tax bill on personal life decisions, is crucial. This understanding can transform the delivery from merely professional to empathetically engaging, recognising the human element in every business interaction.

Lawyers as Emotional Buffers: Lawyers often need to absorb and manage the emotional outputs of clients, who may be in distressing situations. Acting almost as therapists, lawyers dissect and manage these emotions, helping clients focus on the legal aspects of their issues. This role requires understanding the client's core concerns, not just legally but emotionally, and addressing them with both respect and comprehensive legal insight.

The Personal Cost of Legal Practice: Focusing extensively on client needs can lead to personal costs for lawyers, including emotional detachment and reduced empathy. High-stakes environments and the need to suppress emotions can exacerbate this, distancing lawyers from both their own feelings and those of their clients. However, the most effective lawyers manage to integrate empathy into their practice, enhancing trust and communication with clients.

Impact on Lawyers' Mental Health: The demanding nature of legal work, coupled with high stress and constant availability, significantly impacts lawyers' mental health. The pressure to remain responsive and manage a heavy workload without adequate support can lead to burnout and mental health crises within the profession. This environment not only affects productivity but also personal well-being, necessitating a balanced approach to workload management and client expectations.

EXECUTIVE SUMMARY OF PART 3: NEW GENERATION LAW FIRMS

Chapter 7: What does a new generation law firm look like?

This chapter outlines the emergence and characteristics of new generation law firms, which are distinguished by their modern approach to both client relations and work environment. These firms set themselves apart by actively presenting their unique values and vision on platforms like LinkedIn, while effectively positioning themselves in contrast to traditional Big Law practices, particularly criticising their unsustainable demands, such as extreme billing targets.

The chapter highlights how new generation law firms attract like-minded lawyers and clients who value humane working conditions and resonate with the firm's ethos. Such alignment is crucial as many clients in today's legal market are inhouse lawyers with past experiences in private practices, making them more discerning and sensitive to the operational culture and values of law firms.

A significant theme discussed is the client-centric approach adopted by these firms. The narrative emphasises that successful legal service delivery in the current era combines both new technological tools and traditional practices that maintain personal client relationships, especially in complex, high-stakes situations.

The covid-19 pandemic and the integration of AI technology are acknowledged as transformative forces that have shifted traditional interactions and service delivery methods. These changes necessitate a more human-focused approach to offset the distancing effects of technological solutions.

Finally, the chapter argues that new generation law firms excel in building sustainable client relationships not by selling but by engaging meaningfully. They leverage modern communication platforms to relate authentically with clients, moving away from the antiquated, stiff formalities that once dominated the legal industry. This modern approach not only attracts clients but also appeals to a new wave of legal professionals looking for workplaces that champion progressive values and work-life balance.

AI-generated executive summaries

Chapter 8: Phases of AI adoption at law firms

Innovation in private practice is a gradual process, with AI adoption expected to unfold over approximately a decade, reflecting the conservative nature of the legal field. The transition to AI will likely occur in phases, driven by both the introduction of potent technological tools and a shift in operational paradigms.

Short-term Changes: Initially, law firms might see staff reductions as AI tools begin to handle large volumes of document processing, reducing the need for extensive human teams, particularly in low level work. Lawyers will find themselves capable of managing more with fewer personnel, thanks to AI-enhanced data rooms and contracting processes that improve efficiency and accuracy.

Medium-term Responses: As AI tools become more integrated, law firms will need to train all staff in prompt engineering, hire based on AI proficiency, and establish policies for the sustained use of these technologies. These steps will facilitate the gradual replacement of traditional roles with AI systems, leading to significant changes in firm structures and workflows.

Long-term Vision: The long-term response will likely involve law firms developing their proprietary AI models and more deeply reimagining their operational structures. This transformation will aim to optimise the balance between human legal expertise and machine efficiency, ensuring that law firms remain competitive and responsive to client needs in a rapidly evolving digital landscape.

This phased approach underscores the cautious but inevitable integration of AI in legal practices, highlighting a future where technology and human expertise coexist to enhance the delivery of legal services.

Chapter 9: Tasks that will remain with human lawyers

Despite the significant advances in AI, there are core legal tasks that will remain firmly in the domain of human lawyers. This chapter touches upon areas where lawyers' unique human skills are irreplaceable, underscoring the complementarity between AI tools and human legal expertise.

Instruction Quality: Lawyers' daily engagement with complex language makes them naturally proficient in prompt engineering – the art of formulating precise queries that yield useful AI outputs. Just as senior lawyers guide younger colleagues through meticulous instructions, they must similarly finesse AI inputs to achieve desired results. This iterative process between querying and refining outputs is akin to traditional legal mentorship, emphasising the critical role of legal acumen in harnessing AI effectively.

Relationship Building and Management: Beyond technical proficiency, the quintessential human task of forging and nurturing client relationships remains solely with lawyers. The ability to build trust and understand client needs on a personal level cannot be replicated by AI. While the legal industry is crowded with competent practitioners, personal rapport often tips the scales in favour of one law firm over another, highlighting the enduring value of human interaction in legal services.

Understanding Nuances and Ethical Considerations: Lawyers excel in interpreting the nuances of law within its broader context, and incorporating ethical considerations that AI cannot comprehend. This deep contextual and ethical understanding ensures that lawyers can navigate complex legal landscapes more adeptly than AI, which lacks the ability to appreciate the subtleties of human norms and the implications of legal decisions.

Experience and Creativity: Experienced lawyers possess an intuitive grasp of legal matters, enabling them to quickly identify key issues and creative solutions that escape rigid AI algorithms. This seasoned intuition and creativity are crucial in handling complex cases where a standard approach falls short. Furthermore, the human capacity for creative problem-solving and strategic thinking is vital in negotiations and legal strategy, areas where AI tools provide support but cannot lead.

The Future of Human and AI Collaboration: While AI significantly augments a lawyer's capability, particularly in processing information and preliminary data analysis, the essential human qualities of judgement, empathy, and ethical reasoning ensure that the legal profession will continue to rely on its human lawyers. Lawyers are encouraged to embrace AI as a powerful tool for enhancing their practice but remain vigilant about the areas where human oversight is irreplaceable.

Overall, this chapter reinforces the idea that while AI transforms the legal landscape, the essence of legal practice – rooted in human judgement, ethical considerations, and interpersonal relationships – will continue to necessitate a human core, complemented by, but not replaced by, technological advancements.

Appendix 2

List of AI tools useful for lawyers

Below is a list of AI tools useful for lawyers, as available at the time of writing. The list serves as a collection of information gathered from online sources, with the product description of each tool summarised by AI.

This list is not exhaustive but rather a small collection of tools the author is aware of. Many of these tools have been covered elsewhere in the book in more detail. However, in order to retain the relevance of the book, the author has generally refrained from naming particular tools in the chapters of this publication.

In actuality there are many more AI tools available and the reader is encouraged to do their own research to find the tools best suited to their specific needs.

Category: Note takers	
Name	**Product description**
Supernormal	AI–mazing meeting notes. Spend less time writing, polishing, and sharing notes and more time on the work only you can do.
	Key features:
	• Automated note-taking and transcription during meetings.
	• Instant generation of detailed meeting notes and action items.
	• Customizable templates for various meeting types.
	• Seamless integration with Google Meet, Zoom, and Microsoft Teams.
	• Centralised access to all meeting notes.
	Supernormal enhances productivity by allowing users to focus on the conversation while it handles note-taking and formatting automatically.
Fireflies.ai	Fireflies.ai helps your team transcribe, summarise, search, and analyse voice conversations.
	Key features:
	• Automated meeting transcription and note-taking.
	• AI-generated summaries and action items.

List of AI tools useful for lawyers

Fireflies.ai (*contd*)	• Integration with major video conferencing and CRM platforms. • Searchable meeting library. • Collaborative note-editing. Fireflies.ai can join video calls as a virtual participant, recording and transcribing the entire conversation. Its ability to extract action items and key discussion points can help users efficiently follow up on meetings and track progress.
Otter.ai	Never take meeting notes again. Get transcripts, automated summaries, action items, and chat with Otter to get answers from your meetings. Key features: • Real-time transcription and note-taking during video calls. • Speaker identification and attribution. • Automated summary generation. • Searchable transcripts and notes. • Integration with popular video conferencing platforms. Otter.ai can automatically capture and transcribe meetings, allowing participants to focus on the conversation rather than manual note-taking. Its ability to generate summaries and highlight key points can be particularly useful for quickly reviewing meeting outcomes.
Category: Research, analysis, drafting	
ChatGPT	Helps you get answers, find inspiration and be more productive. Free to use. Easy to try. Just ask and ChatGPT can help with writing, learning, brainstorming, and more. Key features: • Natural Language Processing: Chat GPT can understand and generate human-like text, enabling smooth and coherent conversations. • Information Retrieval: It can quickly search through vast amounts of data to provide relevant information, making it useful for research and fact-checking. • Content Generation: The model can assist in drafting emails, reports, and other documents, saving time on routine writing tasks.

List of AI tools useful for lawyers

ChatGPT (*contd*)	• Summarisation: Chat GPT can summarise long texts or complex information, helping professionals digest essential points quickly. • Task Automation: It can automate repetitive tasks, allowing professionals to focus on more strategic activities. • Learning Aid: The model can explain concepts and provide insights on a wide range of topics, serving as a learning companion. • Interactive Q&A: Users can engage in a dialogue, asking follow-up questions to clarify or expand on topics of interest. • Multilingual Capabilities: Chat GPT can communicate in multiple languages, broadening its accessibility for global professionals. These features contribute to increased efficiency and productivity, making Chat GPT a versatile tool for professionals in various sectors.
CoCounsel	Provided by Casetext and powered by Thomson Reuters via Westlaw and Practical Law. Chat-based AI assistant across all professional workflows, making quick work of routine tasks and analysing information. Key features: • Legal Research: CoCounsel can quickly search through case law databases to provide relevant information and answers to legal questions, complete with citations and explanations. • Document Review: The AI can analyse large volumes of documents, such as emails or contracts, to identify specific information or patterns. • Deposition Preparation: CoCounsel can generate thorough deposition outlines based on case details and the deponent's information. • Contract Analysis: It can review contracts line-by-line, answer specific questions about contract contents, and identify clauses that may not comply with given policies.

List of AI tools useful for lawyers

CoCounsel (*contd*)	•	Document Summarisation: CoCounsel can provide concise summaries of legal documents in everyday language.
	•	Legal Writing Assistance: The AI can help draft common legal letters and emails, which can be further refined through interactive chat.
	•	Integration with Legal Workflows: CoCounsel is being integrated into various Thomson Reuters products like Westlaw Precision and Practical Law.
	•	Microsoft 365 Integration: The tool is accessible within Microsoft applications such as Word, Teams, and Outlook.
	•	Document Management System Integration: CoCounsel can access customer documents directly through integrations with systems like iManage, NetDocuments, and SharePoint.
		These features are designed to enhance efficiency and accuracy in various aspects of legal work, from research and document preparation to analysis and client communication.
Claude		Claude is an advanced artificial intelligence assistant developed by Anthropic.
		Key features:
	•	Ability to analyse and summarise lengthy documents.
	•	Multi-task capabilities (writing, coding, analysis, etc.).
	•	Emphasis on AI safety and ethical use.
	•	Multilingual support.
	•	File handling and contextual learning from uploaded documents.
	•	Customisation options for enterprise use.
		Claude can quickly analyse large volumes of legal documents, cases, and statutes to extract key information and insights. This can significantly speed up legal research tasks. Claude can review extensive legal precedents and reference materials to assist in drafting logically consistent and well-aligned legal documents. Claude can further help summarise case facts, identify relevant precedents, and even suggest potential arguments or strategies based on its analysis of similar cases.

List of AI tools useful for lawyers

CoPilot	Copilot is Microsoft's AI assistant that integrates with Microsoft 365 applications like Word, Excel, PowerPoint, Outlook, and Teams. Key features: • Advanced legal research: Copilot can quickly search through case law, statutes, and regulations to find relevant information, generate summaries, and identify key precedents. • Document drafting: The AI can assist in creating first drafts of legal documents, contracts, and communications, saving time on routine writing tasks. • Contract analysis: Copilot can review contracts, suggest edits, identify potential risks, and ensure compliance with legal standards. • Workflow automation: It can automate repetitive tasks, manage documents, and streamline communication within the firm. • Enhanced search capabilities: Copilot can search across the entire Microsoft environment, including emails, documents, and connected external sources, to quickly find relevant information. • Client communication: The AI can help draft personalised client emails and letters, and provide reminders for important tasks and deadlines. • Meeting assistance: Copilot can suggest optimal meeting times based on staff availability and workload, and provide automatic summaries of depositions and hearings. • Compliance support: It can help monitor relevant legal updates and provide timely reminders to ensure compliance with changing regulations.
Gemini	Gemini is an advanced artificial intelligence model developed and provided by Google. It is a multimodal AI system, meaning it can understand and process different types of information including text, images, audio, video, and code. Key Features: • Multimodal capabilities: Gemini can process and understand text, images, audio, and video.

List of AI tools useful for lawyers

Gemini (*contd*)	• Web-based information: Gemini pulls up-to-date information from the web. • Language support: Available in over 40 languages, making it useful for international work. • Research assistance: Gemini can quickly identify relevant concepts, principles, and cases, potentially streamlining research processes. • Document drafting: It can assist in generating first drafts of documents. • Email management: Gemini integrates with Gmail, helping to draft emails, summarise threads, and search through emails efficiently.
Harvey AI	The Trusted Legal AI Platform for Leading Firms. Harvey AI is an innovative tool that utilises a mix of natural language processing and machine learning to support various legal tasks, including contract analysis and litigation support. Key features: • Advanced Research Capabilities: Conduct complex legal research across multiple datasets, including case law and regulations. • Document Analysis and Generation: Draft, analyse, and compare legal documents; generate detailed outlines and provide document Q&A. • Vault Feature: Bulk review and analyse up to 1,000 documents, extracting insights for due diligence. • Assistant Feature: Chat capabilities for legal inquiries; save and load prompts with a character limit of 100,000. • Workflow Integration: Client-matter number integration and orchestration of specialised models for complex tasks. • Security and Compliance: Built on Microsoft Azure with certifications for GDPR, CCPA, and ISO 27001. • Analytics and Productivity Tracking: Monitor firm productivity and track work products by various metrics. • Multilingual Support: Enable work in multiple languages for diverse client needs. These features collectively enhance the efficiency and effectiveness of legal professionals using Harvey AI.

List of AI tools useful for lawyers

LegalFly	The Most Secure Legal AI Workspace. We save your legal teams significant time, reduce your reliance on external lawyers and democratise legal knowledge, giving everyone in your organisation instant access to high quality legal services. Key features: • AI-powered legal document review and analysis. • Significant time savings, reducing contract review time from hours to minutes. • Support for multiple document formats including PDF and Word. • Automated risk identification and missing clause detection. • Contract performance analytics capabilities. • Enhanced data privacy and security through anonymization of personal information. • Subscription-based model providing continuous access to AI advancements. • Streamlined contract negotiations. • Ability to condense and synthesise large amounts of legislation and case law. • Natural language processing allowing lawyers to interact using plain language. • Designed specifically for legal professionals, ensuring more trustworthy and accurate output than general AI models. LegalFly's AI aims to empower legal teams with increased efficiency and accuracy in handling various legal operations, positioning itself as a comprehensive solution for law firms and legal professionals looking to enhance their practices.
Luminance	Your End-to-End Legal AI Co-Pilot. With the ability to produce, analyse and understand content, Luminance's combination of generative and analytical AI ensures the utmost legal rigour. Key features: • Legal-grade AI built on a proprietary Large Language Model (LLM) trained on over 150 million verified legal documents.

List of AI tools useful for lawyers

Luminance (*contd*)	• Cloud-based platform for seamless accessibility and scalability. • Automated contract analysis and mark-up within Microsoft Word. • AI-powered chatbot for legal Q&A and automated contract redrafting. • Intelligent document repository with granular insight capabilities. • Automated contract drafting and process automation tools. • Instant anomaly detection and recognition of over 1,000 out-of-the-box legal concepts. • Automatic clause and document compliance checking.
LexisNexis	LexisNexis has developed AI tools that are effective for answering legal questions and generating memos based on research. It is particularly noted for its comprehensive resources suitable for small firms, offering a range of templates and practical guides for various legal practices. Key features: • Document Drafting: Generates first drafts of legal documents, such as cease and desist letters, which can be further refined by the user. • Document Analysis: Enables users to upload and analyse documents, with the ability to ask questions about the uploaded content. • Source Citation: Generates responses based on LexisNexis' extensive repository of legal sources and provides a list of citations for user review. • Customisation Options: Offers features like setting default jurisdictions and saving conversation history for a more personalised experience. • Security and Privacy: Built with strong security measures to maintain attorney-client privilege and protect sensitive information. These features are designed to streamline legal research, improve document drafting efficiency, and provide lawyers with AI-powered assistance while maintaining the accuracy and reliability crucial in legal work.

List of AI tools useful for lawyers

Perplexity	Perplexity is a free AI-powered answer engine that provides accurate, trusted, and real-time answers to any question. Key features: • Rapid research: Perplexity can quickly process and analyse large volumes of online information, providing concise summaries with relevant citations. • Simplified explanations: The tool can generate clear, concise explanations of complex concepts, improving communication. • PDF analysis: Perplexity's free version allows users to upload and analyse PDF documents, providing quick insights into lengthy texts. • Time-saving: Users report significant time savings, with some users estimating up to 5 hours saved per week on tasks like creating job descriptions and interview criteria. • Fact-checking and verification: While not infallible, Perplexity can be used as a starting point for fact-checking any information. • Up-to-date information: Perplexity provides answers based on current online information.
Category: Contracting	
Juro	Juro is an AI-enhanced contract collaboration platform designed to streamline and automate the entire contract lifecycle for legal teams and businesses. It enables users to create, review, negotiate, sign, and manage contracts more efficiently. Key features: • AI-powered contract drafting and review. • Automated contract templates. • Native eSignature functionality. • Contract analytics and reporting • Secure contract storage and organisation. • Customisable approval workflows. • Automated contract reminders. • Integration with other business tools.

List of AI tools useful for lawyers

Juro (*contd*)	• AI Assistant for faster contract summarisation and analysis. • Collaborative editing and negotiation tools. Juro's AI capabilities help legal teams draft contracts up to 10 times faster than traditional methods. The platform's AI Assistant can summarise contracts, review documents for potential risks, and provide suggestions for revisions based on established guidelines.
Spellbook	Draft contracts 10x faster with AI. Spellbook uses GPT-4 to review and suggest language for your contracts, right in Microsoft Word. Key features: • AI-Powered Contract Drafting: Spellbook uses AI to suggest terms and efficiently draft contracts. • Contract Review and Compliance: The tool helps lawyers review contracts and ensure compliance with relevant regulations. • Redlining Capabilities: Spellbook offers precise redlining based on user instructions, allowing for quick identification of areas of concern. • Language Generation: It can instantly draft new clauses and entire sections based on the context of the agreement. • Aggressive Term Detection: The tool helps identify potentially problematic or unusual terms that may be hidden in contracts. • Missing Clauses and Definitions: Spellbook suggests important language and clauses that may be missing from contracts. • Negotiation Suggestions: It provides insights into common points of negotiation, giving lawyers an edge in contract discussions. • Term Summaries: Spellbook can create short summaries for common contract terms. Spellbook's combination of AI-powered features and integration with familiar software makes it a valuable tool for lawyers looking to streamline their contract drafting and review processes.

List of AI tools useful for lawyers

ContractPodAi	Revolutionising the way legal teams, law firms, and individuals analyse, author, and manage documents on an unprecedented scale. Key features: • Customisable contract templates for efficient creation. • AI-Powered Contract Analytics: Analyses terms and suggests actions using natural language processing. • Smart Repository: Centralised management with powerful search capabilities. • Obligation Tracking: Automated tracking of contract obligations with alerts. • Customisable Workflows: Configurable processes tailored to organisational needs. • Integrated E-Signature: Seamless electronic signature functionality. • Dynamic Reporting and Analytics: Custom reports and a legal dashboard for insights. • Data Security and Compliance: Advanced encryption and adherence to industry standards.
Ironclad	Ironclad provides a platform for legal and business teams to create, store, and manage contracts online in a process known as contract lifecycle management. Key features: • Custom Workflow Design: Streamlines contract creation and management. • Collaborative Editing: Enables simultaneous editing by multiple parties. • Centralised Contract Repository: Provides easy access to all contracts. • AI Playbooks: Alerts users to missing or inappropriate clauses. • AI Assist: Generates redlines for quick acceptance or rejection. • Contract Analytics: Offers real-time visualisation and analysis of contracts. • Integrations: Connects with essential business tools. • Robust Security Features: Protects sensitive contract information.

List of AI tools useful for lawyers

Kira Systems	Kira uses machine learning technology, an application of artificial intelligence, to extract information from your contracts and documents with greater efficiency and accuracy compared to manual review or traditional rules-based systems. Key features: • Automated contract review and analysis using machine learning technology. • Quick extraction and categorisation of important provisions and data points from contracts. • Built-in intelligence with pre-trained models for common legal concepts. • Customizable 'Quick Study' feature allowing users to train the system on specific data points. • Collaborative platform with task assignment and progress tracking capabilities. • Integration with other legal software and applications. • Efficient due diligence process, potentially reducing review time by up to 90% for experienced users. • High accuracy in identifying and extracting relevant information from legal documents. These features enable lawyers to focus on high-value work by automating time-consuming contract review tasks, ultimately improving efficiency and accuracy in legal processes.
Category: Case management	
SisoDiligence	No more M&A risks falling through the cracks. The better way to share and interact with your due diligence findings. Aggregate your due diligence risks, reports and findings from multiple sources into a single collaborative platform. Key features: • Structured Reporting: Utilises a purpose-built Excel template for organised due diligence findings across workstreams. • Findings Tracking: Enables tracking of due diligence findings before and after report finalisation. • Risk-Mitigant Matching: Matches identified risks with proposed mitigants for easy inclusion in internal memos.

List of AI tools useful for lawyers

SisoDiligence (*contd*)	• Transaction Cover Sheet: Captures essential transaction details, including project names and team information. • Key Findings Logging: Logs critical findings with details such as status, risk, and proposed mitigants. • Visual Analytics Dashboard: Provides a snapshot of findings, including risk ratings and unresolved issues. • Customizable Template: Offers flexibility for users to adapt the template to specific due diligence needs.
Clio	Everything your law firm needs. All in one place. Simplify every aspect of your law firm, from billing to communication and document management. Key features: • Case Management: Centralised organisation of case details, documents, and deadlines. • Time Tracking & Billing: Easy recording of billable hours and customised invoicing. • Document Management: Secure cloud storage and organisation of legal documents. • Client Portal: Secure client access to case information and documents. • Calendar & Task Management: Schedule management and task assignment. • Client Intake Forms: Streamlined onboarding with customizable online forms. • CRM Functionality: Lead management and client relationship nurturing. • Online Appointment Booking: Simplified scheduling for client consultations. • Trust Accounting: Compliance management for client trust accounts. • Online Payments: Acceptance of credit card and electronic payments. • Financial Reporting: Insights on firm performance and profitability. • Practice-Specific Tools: Features tailored for various legal practice areas.

List of AI tools useful for lawyers

Whimsical	Tools designed to keep product teams aligned.
	Key features:
	• Diagramming and Flowcharting: Create visual representations of legal processes, case strategies, and complex concepts.
	• Mind Mapping: Organise ideas, break down legal issues, and plan document structures.
	• Collaborative Workspaces: Facilitate real-time collaboration with colleagues and clients, enhancing communication and productivity.
	• Templates and Libraries: Access pre-made templates and legal-specific shapes for efficient diagram creation and reuse.
	These features help lawyers effectively organise information, communicate ideas, and collaborate with ease.
Practice area: Litigation	
Everlaw AI Assistant	Resolve legal matters faster than ever before with generative AI technology built specifically for litigation and investigations.
	Key features:
	• Document summarisation: Quickly creates summaries of single or multiple documents, even for long and complex ones.
	• Sentiment analysis: Analyses and displays positive and negative sentiments expressed in documents.
	• Customised coding suggestions: Provides coding recommendations based on user-defined criteria, with performance comparable to or exceeding human review accuracy.
	• Open-ended document queries: Allows users to ask direct questions about documents and receive on-demand answers with supporting evidence.
	• AI-powered writing assistance: Helps generate first drafts of statements of facts, arguments, or interview summaries with built-in citations.
	• Batch processing: Enables summarisation, information extraction, and coding suggestions across thousands of documents simultaneously.
	These features are designed to accelerate document review, improve understanding of case materials, and enhance overall productivity in litigation and investigations workflows.

List of AI tools useful for lawyers

Lex Machina	Leveraging the latest advances in computer science together with our in-house legal expertise, Lex Machina has created a unique Legal Analytics Platform that enables you to craft successful strategies, win cases, and close business. Key features: • Comprehensive Legal Analytics: In-depth insights on courts, judges, lawyers, and law firms. • Motion Metrics: Historical outcomes for various motion types in specific courts. • Case List Analyzer: Detailed timelines and connections of case documents and filings. • Attorney and Law Firm Intelligence: Performance metrics and experience of opposing counsel and firms. • Damages Analytics: Information on damages awarded in past cases for valuation strategies.
Practice area: Tax	
Blue J	Generative AI for tax experts. Experience a new era of tax technology that delivers fast, verifiable answers to your tax questions, empowering you to work smarter and more efficiently. Key features: • AI-powered outcome prediction with 90% accuracy. • Rapid case finding, locating relevant decisions 100 times faster than traditional methods. • Automated report generation with findings. • Machine learning algorithms to identify patterns in judicial rulings. • Analysis of employment law issues like reasonable notice and worker classification. • Comprehensive sourcing of tax law materials, including statutes, regulations, and case law. • Ability to generate memos and client emails summarising research findings. Blue J aims to streamline legal research and analysis, particularly in areas like tax and employment law, by leveraging artificial intelligence to provide faster and more accurate insights for legal professionals.

List of AI tools useful for lawyers

Category: Brand	
Copy.ai	Solution for enterprise marketing teams looking to improve their go-to-market strategy and streamline their content. Key features: • Content Generation Tools: Copy.ai provides over 90 templates for various content types, including blog posts, social media updates, product descriptions, and ad copy, allowing users to quickly generate high-quality text. • Blog Post Wizard: This feature helps users create complete blog posts, including outlines and titles, significantly reducing the time needed to draft content. • Brand Voice and Infobase Features: These functionalities enable users to maintain a consistent brand tone and store essential company information for easy access during content creation, enhancing efficiency and coherence in messaging.
Jasper.ai	Tap into a central nervous system for all your content with Jasper's Brand Voice, Knowledge Base & Style Guide. Key features: • Content Generation: Jasper can produce various types of content, including blog posts, social media captions, and long-form articles, based on user prompts and input. • Templates: The platform includes over 50 templates tailored for different content types such as ads, SEO, emails, and social media, facilitating quick content creation. • Tone of Voice Settings: Users can customise the tone of the generated content by defining specific tone descriptors, allowing for personalised and brand-aligned messaging. • Plagiarism Checker: An integrated tool that checks content for originality, helping users ensure that their writing is unique, although this feature may incur additional costs. • Analytics & Insights: The platform offers analytics to help users track the performance of their content, allowing for data-driven adjustments and improvements.

List of AI tools useful for lawyers

Rytr	AI Writer, Content Generator & Writing Assistant. Key features: - AI Writer: Generates original content based on user input, supporting over 30 languages and various tones to match different writing styles. - Plagiarism Checker: Includes an in-built tool to check for duplicate content across the web. - Image Generator: Allows users to create images to accompany their text. - Outline & Brief Generator: Helps users create structured outlines and briefs for their writing projects.
QuillBot	Your ideas, better writing. We use AI to strengthen writing and boost productivity – without sacrificing authenticity. Key features: - Paraphrasing Tool: QuillBot's core feature allows users to rewrite text while maintaining the original meaning. It includes multiple modes such as Standard, Fluency, Formal, and Creative, enabling tailored outputs for different writing styles. - Grammar Checker: This feature identifies grammatical errors and awkward phrasing, ensuring that the text is polished and clear. It integrates seamlessly with the paraphrasing tool. - Plagiarism Checker: QuillBot scans text against a vast database to detect potential plagiarism, helping users ensure their work is original. - Summariser: The summarisation tool condenses text into key points or a brief paragraph, making it easier to distil essential information. - Tone Adjustment: Users can select different tones for their writing, such as casual or formal, to better align with their intended audience. - Multilingual Support: QuillBot supports paraphrasing in 23 languages, making it accessible to a wider range of users. - Extensions: QuillBot offers browser extensions for Google Chrome and Microsoft Word, allowing users to utilise its features directly within their preferred writing environments.

Index

[*all references are to page number*]

Adoption of AI
  advice to young lawyers, 131—132
  cost of staff × cost of AI tools, 92—93
  custom solutions for clients, 103—104
  data pool
    bridge to technical solution, 101—103
    generally, 99—100
  drafting contracts, 91—92
  first responder assistant, 104—106
  fitness for legal work, 94—95
  'hallucination' issue, 94
  human × machine
    numbers, 92—93
    risk profile, 89—91
  implementation of use of tools, 96
  introduction, 85
  law firms, by, 81—82
  long term, in
    approach to training an AI tool, 99—103
    bridge between data pool and technical solution, 101—103
    custom solutions for clients, 103—104
    data pool, 99—100
    first responder assistant, 104—106
    introduction, 97—98
    phases of implementation, 98
    'pull work' system, 106—107, 108—109
    'push work' system, 107—108
    technical solution, 100—101
    training an AI tool, 98—104
  phases, 96—97

Adoption of AI – *contd*
  push-pull work systems
    interaction, 108—109
    'pull work', 106—107
    'push work', 107—108
  quality of tools, 94
  risk profile, 89—91
  safety of tools, 95—96
  short term, in
    cost of staff × cost of AI tools, 92—93
    drafting contracts, 91—92
    fitness for legal work, 94—95
    'hallucination' issue, 94
    human × machine, 89—91, 92—93
    implementation of use of tools, 96
    introduction, 85
    phases, 96—97
    quality, 94
    risk profile, 89—91
    safety of tools, 95—96
    source data linkage, 94
    tactical responses by firm, 93—94
    usefulness of tools, 94—95
  source data linkage, 94
  technical solution
    bridge to data pool, 101—103
    generally, 100—101
  training an AI tool
    approach, 99—103
    bridge between data pool and technical solution, 101—103
    data pool, 99—100
    introduction, 98
    phases of implementation, 98
    technical solution, 100—101

Index

Adoption of AI – *contd*
  trust in lawyer, and, 9—11
  usefulness of AI tools, 94—95
  young lawyers, by, 131—132
Analysis of the law
  data processing, 43—44
Anxiety
  empathy towards clients, 61
Asking questions
  empathy towards clients, 57—58
Assistance by AI
  communication with lawyers, 19—20
  cost savings, 24—25
  data processing, 44—54
  empathy towards clients, 64—68
  language use, 38—42
  processing of data, 44—54
  reliance on lawyer, 19—20
  trust in lawyer, 9—11

Billing of work
  See also **Cost savings**
  AI-generated work, 25
  analysis by AI, 26—27
  models, 21—22
'Blank page block'
  use of language, 38—39
Blockchain
  generally, 79—80
Brain function
  data processing, 43
Branding
  future of law firms, 74—75
Building relationships
  future of law firms, 73—74

Calmness
  empathy towards clients, 55
Case management
  adoption of AI at law firms, 110—111
Clarity of answers
  reliance on lawyer, 16—17
Clarity of communications
  future of law firms, 72—73
  reliance on lawyer, 15—16
Clarity of drafting
  use of language, 35—37

Client's needs
  introduction, 1
  reliance on lawyer
    assistance of AI, 19—20
    clarity of answers, 16—17
    clarity of communications, 15—16
    core client requirement, 13—16
    introduction, 13
    position of client, 13—14
    provision of clear answers, 16—17
    provision of support to client, 16—19
    purpose of legal support, 14—15
    refining the message, 20
    retention of working papers, 18—19
    status updates, 19
    tailoring advice to needs of client, 17—18
  saving of costs
    analysis of client bills by AI, 26—27
    assistance of AI, 24—25
    billing of AI-generated work, 25
    billing models, 21—22
    budget of client, 21
    impact of AI, 25
    introduction, 21
    position of client, 21
    provision of information to client, 24
    value proposition, 23
    win-win arrangements, 23—24
  stress, and, 4—5
  trust in lawyer
    assistance of AI, 9—11
    building trust, 5—9
    communication, 6—7
    effective completion of work, 10—11
    interpersonal skills, 3
    introduction, 3—4
    low-level tasks, 9—10
    mutually beneficial relationships, 7—8
    position of client, 4—5
    prioritising human interaction, 11
    responsiveness, 6

Index

Client's needs – *contd*
  trust in lawyer – *contd*
    restoration when broken, 8—9
    time savings, 9—10
Communication with lawyers
  assistance of AI, 19—20
  clarity of answers, 16—17
  clarity of communications, 15—16
  core client requirement, 13—16
  future of law firms, 72—73
  introduction, 13
  legal support to client
    provision, 16—19
    purpose, 14—15
  position of client, 13—14
  provision of clear answers, 16—17
  provision of support to client, 16—19
  purpose of legal support, 14—15
  refining the message, 20
  retention of working papers, 18—19
  status updates, 19
  tailoring advice to needs of client, 17—18
  trust in lawyer, and, 5—7
Complexity
  use of language, 34—37
Contracts and agreements
  use of language, 40—41
Cost savings
  analysis of client bills by AI, 26—27
  assistance of AI, 24—25
  billing of AI-generated work, 25
  billing models, 21—22
  budget of client, 21
  impact of AI, 25
  introduction, 21
  position of client, 21
  provision of information to client, 24
  value proposition, 23
  win-win arrangements, 23—24
Cost of staff
  implementation of AI, 92—93
Creativity
  future role of lawyers, 117—118
Custom solutions
  implementation of AI, 103—104

Data pool
  bridge to technical solution, 101—103
  generally, 99—100
Data processing
  analysis of the law, 43—44
  brain function, 43
  depositions, 52—53
  discovery, 52—53
  dispute resolution, 54
  drafting contracts, 48—50
  drafting documents, 43—44
  introduction, 43
  language models, 44
  legal analysis, 43—44
  litigation, 51—52
  project management, 50—51
  research, 45—48
  transcribing meetings, 44—45
  use of AI tools, 44—54
  workings of human brain, 43
Decentralised networks
  adoption of AI at law firms, 79—80
Depositions
  data processing, 52—53
Difficult messages
  empathy towards clients, 55—57
Discovery
  data processing, 52—53
Dispute resolution
  data processing, 54
Drafting contracts
  data processing, 48—50
  implementation of AI, 91—92
Drafting documents
  data processing, 43—44

Effective completion of work
  trust in lawyer, 10—11
Empathy towards clients
  anxiety, 61
  asking questions, 57—58
  being calm, 55
  being constantly 'on', 60—61
  client expectations, 63—64
  day-in-the-life of a lawyer, 61—62
  difficult messages, 55—57
  empathy, 55—64

Index

Empathy towards clients – *contd*
  first responder solutions, 67—68
  introduction, 55
  listening, 57—58
  mental health issues, 58—60
  personal cost to lawyers, 58
  respect for client, 57—58
  speed of reply, 66—67
  tone of the message, 64—66
  understanding client's core issue, 57—58
  use of AI tools, 64—68
Ethics
  future role of lawyers, 117
Expectations of client
  empathy towards clients, 63—64
Expertise
  future role of lawyers, 117—118

First response
  empathy towards clients, 67—68
  implementation of AI, 104—106

'Hallucination' issue
  implementation of AI, 94
Human interaction
  trust in lawyer, 11

Implementation of AI
  cost of staff × cost of AI tools, 92—93
  custom solutions for clients, 103—104
  data pool
    bridge to technical solution, 101—103
    generally, 99—100
  drafting contracts, 91—92
  first responder assistant, 104—106
  fitness for legal work, 94—95
  'hallucination' issue, 94
  human × machine
    numbers, 92—93
    risk profile, 89—91
  introduction, 85
  long term, in
    approach to training an AI tool, 99—103

Implementation of AI – *contd*
  long term, in – *contd*
    bridge between data pool and technical solution, 101—103
    custom solutions for clients, 103—104
    data pool, 99—100
    first responder assistant, 104—106
    introduction, 97—98
    phases of implementation, 98
    'pull work' system, 106—107, 108—109
    'push work' system, 107—108
    technical solution, 100—101
    training an AI tool, 98—104
  phases, 96—97
  push-pull work systems
    interaction, 108—109
    'pull work', 106—107
    'push work', 107—108
  quality of tools, 94
  risk profile, 89—91
  safety of tools, 95—96
  short term, in
    cost of staff × cost of AI tools, 92—93
    drafting contracts, 91—92
    fitness for legal work, 94—95
    'hallucination' issue, 94
    human × machine, 89—91, 92—93
    implementation of use of tools, 96
    introduction, 85
    phases, 96—97
    quality, 94
    risk profile, 89—91
    safety of tools, 95—96
    source data linkage, 94
    tactical responses by firm, 93—94
    usefulness of tools, 94—95
  source data linkage, 94
  technical solution
    bridge to data pool, 101—103
    generally, 100—101
  training an AI tool
    approach, 99—103
    bridge between data pool and technical solution, 101—103
    data pool, 99—100

Index

Implementation of AI – *contd*
  training an AI tool – *contd*
    introduction, 98
    phases of implementation, 98
    technical solution, 100—101
    usefulness of AI tools, 94—95
Infinite use cases
  use of language, 41—42
Internet
  adoption of AI at law firms, 76
Interpersonal skills
  trust in lawyer, 3

Language models
  data processing, 44
Language use
  'blank page block', 38—39
  clear drafting, 35—36
  complexity, 34—37
  contracts and agreements, 40—41
  helpful approaches, 37—38
  infinite use cases, 41—42
  introduction, 33—34
  risk sensitivity, 37—38
  'template fallacy', 39—40
  unclear drafting, 36
  use of AI tools, 38—42
  writing style, 34—35
Law firms
  See also **Lawyers**
  adoption of AI
    introduction, 85
    long term view, 97—113
    short-term changes, 85—97
  adoption of AI in long term
    approach to training an AI tool, 99—103
    bridge between data pool and technical solution, 101—103
    custom solutions for clients, 103—104
    data pool, 99—100
    first responder assistant, 104—106
    introduction, 97—98
    phases of implementation, 98
    'pull work' system, 106—107, 108—109

Law firms – *contd*
  adoption of AI in long term – *contd*
    'push work' system, 107—108
    technical solution, 100—101
    training an AI tool, 98—104
  adoption of AI in short term
    cost of staff × cost of AI tools, 92—93
    drafting contracts, 91—92
    fitness for legal work, 94—95
    'hallucination' issue, 94
    human × machine, 89—91, 92—93
    implementation of use of tools, 96
    introduction, 85
    phases of implementation, 96—97
    quality, 94
    risk profile, 89—91
    safety of tools, 95—96
    source data linkage, 94
    tactical responses by firm, 93—94
    usefulness of tools, 94—95
  approach to the client, 71—72
  approach to legal staff, 76—77
  blockchain, 79—80
  branding, 74—75
  building relationships, 73—74
  case management, 110—111
  communication with the client, 72—73
  custom solutions, 103—104
  decentralised networks, 79—80
  first responder assistant, 104—106
  future structure, 111—113
  implementation of AI
    long term view, 97—113
    methodology, 71—83
    phases, 85—113
    short-term changes, 85—97
  internet, 76
  introduction, 69
  'look-and-feel', 71—83
  privacy concerns, 80
  push-pull work systems
    interaction, 108—109
    'pull work', 106—107
    'push work', 107—108
  role of lawyers
    context, 117

Index

Law firms – *contd*
  role of lawyers – *contd*
    creativity, 117—118
    ethics, 117
    expertise, 117—118
    introduction, 115—116
    management, 116
    marketing and sales, 120—121
    negotiations, 118—120
    nuance, 117
    problem solving, 118—120
    relationship building, 116
    strategizing, 118—120
  security concerns, 80
  servicing all client needs, 75—76
  social media, 79
  technological innovation, 76—78
  training an AI tool
    approach, 99—103
    bridge between data pool and technical solution, 101—103
    data pool, 99—100
    introduction, 98
    phases of implementation, 98
    technical solution, 100—101
  use of AI, 81—82
  Web 3, 78—81
  'winning', 109—110
  working with AI, 82—83

Lawyers
  advice to
    alternative career paths, 127—128
    client service mindset, 126—127
    'find your field', 125—126
    helpfulness, 124—125
    increasing expertise, 130—131
    introduction, 123
    'law firm trap', 128—129
    learn from the best, 123—124
    legal career outside law firms, 130
    navigating in uncertain terrain, 132—134
    partnership goal, 129
    reflection, 127
    'specialist trap', 128—129
    use of AI, 131—132
  AI tools, 31—32

Lawyers – *contd*
  data processors, as
    analysis of the law, 43—44
    brain function, 43
    depositions, 52—53
    discovery, 52—53
    dispute resolution, 54
    drafting contracts, 48—50
    drafting documents, 43—44
    introduction, 43
    language models, 44
    legal analysis, 43—44
    litigation, 51—52
    project management, 50—51
    research, 45—48
    transcribing meetings, 44—45
    use of AI tools, 44—54
    workings of human brain, 43
  future role
    context, 117
    creativity, 117—118
    ethics, 117
    expertise, 117—118
    introduction, 115—116
    management, 116
    marketing and sales, 120—121
    negotiations, 118—120
    nuance, 117
    problem solving, 118—120
    relationship building, 116
    strategizing, 118—120
  introduction, 29—31
  language engineers, as
    'blank page block', 38—39
    clear drafting, 35—36
    complexity, 34—37
    contracts and agreements, 40—41
    helpful approaches, 37—38
    infinite use cases, 41—42
    introduction, 33—34
    risk sensitivity, 37—38
    'template fallacy', 39—40
    unclear drafting, 36
    use of AI tools, 38—42
    writing style, 34—35
  therapists, as
    anxiety, 61

Index

Lawyers – *contd*
  therapists, as – *contd*
    asking questions, 57—58
    being calm, 55
    being constantly 'on', 60—61
    client expectations, 63—64
    day-in-the-life of a lawyer, 61—62
    difficult messages, 55—57
    empathy, 55—64
    first responder solutions, 67—68
    introduction, 55
    listening, 57—58
    mental health issues, 58—60
    personal cost to lawyers, 58
    respect for client, 57—58
    speed of reply, 66—67
    tone of the message, 64—66
    understanding client's core issue, 57—58
    use of AI tools, 64—68
Legal analysis
  data processing, 43—44
Legal support to client
  provision, 16—19
  purpose, 14—15
Listening
  empathy towards clients, 57—58
Litigation
  data processing, 51—52
Low-level tasks
  trust in lawyer, 9—10

Management
  future role of lawyers, 116
Marketing and sales
  future role of lawyers, 120—121
Mental health issues
  empathy towards clients, 58—60
Mutually beneficial relationships
  trust in lawyer, 7—8

Negotiations
  future role of lawyers, 118—120
Nuance
  future role of lawyers, 117

Practice-specific work
  AI tools, 31

Privacy
  adoption of AI at law firms, 80
Problem solving
  future role of lawyers, 118—120
Processing data
  analysis of the law, 43—44
  brain function, 43
  depositions, 52—53
  discovery, 52—53
  dispute resolution, 54
  drafting contracts, 48—50
  drafting documents, 43—44
  introduction, 43
  language models, 44
  legal analysis, 43—44
  litigation, 51—52
  project management, 50—51
  research, 45—48
  transcribing meetings, 44—45
  use of AI tools, 44—54
  workings of human brain, 43
Productivity
  AI tools, 31
Project management
  data processing, 50—51
Provision of information
  cost of work, 24
Push-pull work systems
  interaction, 108—109
  'pull work', 106—107
  'push work', 107—108

Quality
  implementation of AI, 94

Relationship building
  future role of lawyers, 116
Reliance on lawyer
  assistance of AI, 19—20
  clarity of answers, 16—17
  clarity of communications, 15—16
  core client requirement, 13—16
  introduction, 13
  legal support to client
    provision, 16—19
    purpose, 14—15
  position of client, 13—14

173

Index

Reliance on lawyer – *contd*
   provision of clear answers, 16—17
   provision of support to client, 16—19
   purpose of legal support, 14—15
   refining the message, 20
   retention of working papers, 18—19
   status updates, 19
   tailoring advice to needs of client, 17—18

Research
   data processing, 45—48
   trust in lawyer, and, 9—10

Respect for client
   empathy towards clients, 57—58

Responsiveness
   trust in lawyer, 6

Retention of working papers
   reliance on lawyer, 18—19

Retention of working papers
   reliance on lawyer, 18—19

Risk profile
   implementation of AI, 89—91
   use of language, 37—38

Safety
   implementation of AI, 95—96

Security
   adoption of AI at law firms, 80

Social media
   adoption of AI at law firms, 79

Source data
   implementation of AI, 94

Speed of reply
   empathy towards clients, 66—67

Status updates
   communication with lawyers, 19

Strategising
   future role of lawyers, 118—120

Stress of client
   trust in lawyer, 72—73

Technological innovation
   adoption of AI at law firms, 76—78

Therapeutic approaches
   anxiety, 61
   asking questions, 57—58
   being calm, 55

Therapeutic approaches – *contd*
   being constantly 'on', 60—61
   client expectations, 63—64
   day-in-the-life of a lawyer, 61—62
   difficult messages, 55—57
   empathy, 55—64
   first responder solutions, 67—68
   introduction, 55
   listening, 57—58
   mental health issues, 58—60
   personal cost to lawyers, 58
   respect for client, 57—58
   speed of reply, 66—67
   tone of the message, 64—66
   understanding client's core issue, 57—58
   use of AI tools, 64—68

'Template fallacy'
   use of language, 39—40

Time savings
   trust in lawyer, 9—10

Tone of the message
   empathy towards clients, 64—66

Training an AI tool
   approach, 99—103
   bridge between data pool and technical solution, 101—103
   data pool, 99—100
   introduction, 98
   phases of implementation, 98
   technical solution, 100—101

Transcribing meetings
   data processing, 44—45

Trust in lawyer
   assistance of AI, 9—11
   building trust, 5—9
   communication, 6—7
   effective completion of work, 10—11
   interpersonal skills, 3
   introduction, 3—4
   low-level tasks, 9—10
   mutually beneficial relationships, 7—8
   position of client, 4—5
   prioritising human interaction, 11
   responsiveness, 6
   restoration when broken, 8—9
   time savings, 9—10

Index

Understanding client's issues
  empathy towards clients, 57—58
Use of language
  assistance of AI, 38—42
  'blank page block', 38—39
  clear drafting, 35—36
  complexity, 34—37
  contracts and agreements, 40—41
  helpful approaches, 37—38
  infinite use cases, 41—42
  introduction, 33—34
  risk sensitivity, 37—38
  'template fallacy', 39—40
  unclear drafting, 36
  use of AI tools, 38—42

Use of language – *contd*
  writing style, 34—35
Usefulness
  implementation of AI, 94—95

Value proposition
  cost savings, 23

Web 3
  future of law firms, 78—81
Win-win arrangements
  cost savings, 23—24
Workings of human brain
  data processing, 43
Writing style
  use of language, 34—35